Unlocking the Language of Dreams

LUC NIEBERGALL

Copyright © 2016 by Luc Niebergall

All rights reserved. This book or any portion thereof may not be reproduced or used in any manner whatsoever without the express written permission of the publisher except for the use of brief quotations in a book review.

Printed in the United States of America

First Edition, 2016

ISBN-10: 1537760688
ISBN-13: 978-1537760681

Royal Identity Ministries

Table of Content

The Foundation of Dreams…………………………………….…7

Receiving from God in the Night Season……….....……..19

The Vast Array of Dreams……………………………………..31

Interpreting Symbols…………………………….....………….57

Dream Interpretation Dictionary……………………....…….71

The Foundation of Dreams

The Lord is calling His Bride, the church, to know Him in friendship and intimacy. God, who created the earth in all of its intricacies, the stars in all of their majesty, and the universe in all of its enormity, desires above all things to know you as a friend. As you journey through life experiencing seasons of great triumphs, times of trials, seasons of promotion and periods of testing, God is on His own journey. He is venturing down the road of your soul to encounter the core of your heart. He is inviting you on a journey, leading you from a place of surface-level understanding, into the mysteries of who He is.

Unlocking the Language of Dreams

A fundamental key to knowing the Lord as a friend is understanding how He speaks. Communication is an irreplaceable aspect in relationships. God wants to broaden our capacity to understand His language. God's expression of language is not miniscule, but diverse. We know that the Lord can speak prophetically in a variety of ways. He can speak in ways that are subtle; through the still small quiet voice, through visions, or through our family and friends. He can also speak in ways that are dramatic, like when He utters the mysteries of His heart through the vastness of His creation. He communicates in ways that are practical, such as with wise council; as well as in supernatural and mystical ways, for instance when He speaks through His messengers, the angels. There is not a particular mould in how He speaks, because He is not mechanical in nature, but organic. He can speak however He chooses. A very significant way that the Lord does speak, which I believe has in many ways been forgotten, is through the language of dreams.

Job 33:15-16: "In a dream, in a vision of the night, when deep sleep falls upon men, while slumbering on their beds, then He opens the ears of men, and seals their instruction."

The Foundation of Dreams

Not only are dreams a way that God speaks, but they are also an avenue for God to communicate both His love and His instruction to us.

Every morning before our day begins, my wife and I ask one another the question, "What did you dream?" We do this not only because we both have unbelievably active dream lives, but also because it is in the night season that the Lord prophesies the word of the Lord to us to seal our instruction. My wife and I receive much of our direction in life through what God communicates to us in our dreams.

A few years ago, my wife and I were in a very interesting season of transition. At that time, we had been walking in a high level leadership position alongside a specific ministry for a few years, when we felt like the Lord was moving us onward to new things. Since we were so highly invested in this ministry, we were trying to correctly discern whether this was in fact the Lord moving us on. As we were in process about the transition we were feeling in our hearts, the Lord gave me a dream.

In this dream, my wife and I were driving in a car down a highway. To our left, driving in a separate car, was the key leader of this ministry who we had been walking with. All of a sudden, we saw a sign on the side of the road that said there was a highway exit coming up. Immediately, I felt like the Lord said that we needed to take that turn off. We then took the next turn off and waved goodbye to the leader, who kept driving straight. That was the entire dream.

We felt as though this was a very clear dream. Vehicles in a dream will often symbolize a ministry. The interpretation of the dream was that my wife and I had been called to walk alongside this ministry for a season, but the Lord was moving us on. I held onto this dream as confirmation of what we had been sensing the Lord was declaring.

A few weeks after having this dream, I was having coffee with a highly gifted prophetic minister. We were chatting, when all of a sudden in mid-conversation, he began to tell me that the Lord was showing him something for me.

He said, "The Lord just showed me a vision of you. I saw you driving with your wife in a car down a highway. On your left, there was a car driving beside you." The man then named the person in the car, and it was the leader who was in my dream. "In the vision, you saw an exit sign and the Lord told you to take the next turn off. As you took the turn off, you waved to the other driver saying goodbye." It was amazing how the Lord used this dream and prophetic word to confirm to me the direction of the Lord in my life.

The Foundation of Dreams

I believe that God is wanting to broaden our capacity to hear Him. This includes hearing Him in the night season. When we think about the different ways that God speaks, we might assume that dreams are one of the more far-fetched ways that God would use to communicate to us. Many of us assume that hearing God speak through dreams is only for some, and not all. However, considering how much time we spend sleeping, this could not be further from the truth. We spend approximately one third of our lives sleeping. This means that if you live to be 90 years old, you will have slept for approximately 30 years of your life.

If we entertain the belief that God does not want to speak to us through dreams in the night season, we essentially establish a wall of doubt within our hearts, believing that God does not want to speak to us for one third of our lives. God desires to cultivate such a close friendship with us, where we are in constant communion with Him. He wants us to be continually receiving His word, love and affirmation.

All throughout the Old Testament we can see that it was very common for God to speak through dreams.

1 Samuel 28:6: "When Saul inquired of the LORD, the LORD did not answer him, either by dreams or by

Urim or by the prophets."

This tells us that when King Saul was waiting for the word of the Lord, he expected it to come through either the prophets of Israel, or through a dream. In the Old Testament, kings expected that the Lord would speak to them through dreams, giving them instruction in how to lead their kingdoms. We can also see this with governmental leaders such as Pharaoh in Genesis 41 and King Nebuchadnezzar in Daniel 2. It was common knowledge during this time period that the Lord spoke through dreams, to the point where it was expected. Not only was it expected, but it was a key source of decision making for people of influence.

Matthew 2:13: "Now when they (Joseph, Mary and Jesus) had departed, behold, an angel of the Lord appeared to Joseph in a dream, saying, 'Arise, take the young Child and His mother, flee to Egypt, and stay there until I bring you word; for Herod will seek the young Child to destroy Him.'"

Mary and Joseph were given the profound responsibility of parenting and raising Jesus while He was a child. Based on what we can see in scripture, it seems as though Mary was entrusted to nurture Jesus; whereas, Joseph's role was to hear and listen to

The Foundation of Dreams

the word of God in order to stand as Jesus' protector. While Joseph lived out this important mandate, one of the primary ways God chose to guide Him was through the use of dreams. Joseph had to have his ears attuned to hear the word of the Lord even in the season of the night, in order to fulfill the mandate over his life.

I have heard many argue, saying that God spoke through dreams in the Old Testament, however, now in New Testament times we no longer need God to speak through dreams because we have Holy Spirit. This sounds logical; however, it is unbiblical. Look at this:

Acts 2:17-18: "This is what was spoken by the prophet Joel: 'And it shall come to pass in the last days, says God, that I will pour out of My Spirit on all flesh; your sons and your daughters shall prophesy, your young men shall see visions, your old men shall dream dreams.'"

Given that the Spirit of God has been poured out, this verse tells us that dreams should actually be increasing! If God spoke through dreams in the Old Testament, then through the cross, our access to the voice of God should be heightened all the more.

Unlocking the Language of Dreams

In my ministry, we have seen God use dreams as a way to minister to those who do not yet know Jesus. I have, on many occasions while just going about my day, met people who have been puzzled by dreams they have had. This has given me the opportunity to interpret their dream and share with them the word of the Lord for their lives in their current season. The result is that they will often give their lives to the Lord.

I remember one time, while I was walking throughout a bookstore, I felt the Lord highlight to me two teenagers who were in the New Age section. They were looking through a book on dream interpretation that was clearly rooted in the occult. Walking up to them, I said, "It looks like you two need a dream interpreted."

One of the teenagers piped up telling me that she had a dream a few nights before and that she couldn't get it out of her head. I offered to interpret the dream if she would be willing to share it with me.

The teenager told me her dream, saying, "In my dream, I was running away from different people who I am in relationship with. This caused me to run into a dark forest. In the forest, I was looking for light, but I could not find it."

The Foundation of Dreams

Holy Spirit began to reveal to me the interpretation of the dream. He showed me there were people in her life that she was in relationship with who made her feel unsafe. She was looking for fulfillment in those relationships, but this was causing her to go into a dark place in her heart, resulting in depression. I was then able to share with her that the light she was looking for was Jesus, and that even though she hadn't seen Him in the dream, He wanted to come live in those hurting places in her heart.

This young woman had a profound encounter with the love of God that day. As God touched her heart in the bookstore, she cried as Jesus came to dwell in her heart, freeing her from confusion and depression.

Probably the most common question I am asked concerning dreams is this: "Is every dream from God?" In short answer, no, not every dream is from God. Some dreams are from God, some are from the enemy, and others are because we had pizza before we went to bed.

A good measure of whether or not a dream is from God, is if the dream firmly sticks with you. The Hebrew word for "dream" means "to bind firmly". When we have a dream from the Lord, it is because He is trying to bind a message firmly to our heart. We can see this with the testimony that you just read

Unlocking the Language of Dreams

about the teenager in the book store. God speaks with authority, so when He speaks in a dream it will often be bound to our heart.

God wants us to grasp the revelation that He desires to speak to each of us. Not only does He want to speak to us, but He wants to open up communication with us in the diverse ways that He speaks. For some of you reading, you may already have a consistent dream life. Others of you may have had many dreams filled with symbols that you do not yet understand. Still, others may not have any dream life at all. No matter what category you fall into, I believe that God wants to open up communication with you in the night season, so that you are in constant communion with Him. God wants to unlock the language of dreams in your life.

To end this chapter, I want to take time to pray with you, that God will stir faith in you that He does indeed still speak through dreams. Feel free to position yourself with the Lord right now to receive what He has for you.

"Holy Spirit, I pray right now that You will increase faith in Your child that You want to speak to them. Stir in them a revelation that You are so ravished by them that You want to be in constant communion with them. I pray right now that You

The Foundation of Dreams

would begin to open up their spirit and soul in the night season. I pray for an impartation from Your heart to understand Your voice through dreams."

I would encourage you to look up and meditate on the following scriptures to boost your faith regarding dreams:

Genesis 20:3-7	Daniel 2:1
Genesis 28:12	Daniel 4:5
Genesis 31:10	Daniel 4:8
Genesis 31:24	Daniel 7
Genesis 37:5-9	Matthew 1:20
Genesis 40:5:19	Matthew 2:13
Genesis 41:1-7	Matthew 2:11-12
Judges 7:13-15	Matthew 2:19-20
1 Kings 3:5-15	Matthew 27:19

Receiving from God in the Night Season

In the secular world, Sigmund Freud was the pioneer of the theory that dreams are an expression of man's inner being communicating with the mind. He taught that we subconsciously tell ourselves through our dreams if there are problems or issues that we need to resolve. The Bible teaches that our dream lives are an avenue that God uses to speak to us.

I believe that it is God's heart to speak to all of His children through dreams, although the frequency may vary considering that God's relationship with each of us is wonderfully unique. I know some highly prophetic leaders who have extremely active dream lives, such as I do, where for others it is not as common. However, I do believe that it is God's heart that we all will be able to receive from Him in some capacity through the avenue of dreams.

This poses the question: If God wants to speak to us through dreams, why is it that some dream, and others do not?

There could be a few reasons why some people do not have dream lives. The following are some of the reasons I have discovered:

Lack of Expectation

The first reason why we may not experience God speak to us through dreams is simply due to a lack of expectancy that God actually wants to speak to us in this way.

I have taught many schools about the prophetic ministry and how to hear the voice of God. Something that I have observed is that when I train specifically relating to dreams, people's dream lives begin to increase as they receive a basic knowledge that the Lord desires to speak to them in this way. It was not that they had a blockage preventing them from hearing through dreams. They simply did not know that it was possible.

Remember in John 12 when Jesus was teaching parables to a group of people? In verse 28 and 29 Jesus says, "'Father, glorify Your name.' Then a voice came from heaven, saying, 'I have both glorified it and will glorify it again.' Therefore, the people who stood by and heard it said that it had thundered. Others said, 'An angel has spoken to Him.'"

We need to catch this. A voice came down from heaven and spoke audibly, but only some heard a voice, whereas others only heard thunder. What was the difference between those who heard the voice and those who heard thunder? Some had positioned their hearts to hear the word of the Lord in whichever way God chose to speak. The others did not. It was their level of expectation that determined whether or not they heard God speak.

We need to be open to hearing the Lord speak to us in whichever way He chooses. We often do not encounter the voice of the Lord in different and abstract ways, simply because we do not expect it. However, God wants to expand our faith concerning that He does indeed want to speak to us. The more we begin to expect the Lord to speak to us through dreams, the more it permits communication to increase in this avenue of God's language toward us.

Unlocking the Language of Dreams

If you are looking to increase your dream life, I would recommend keeping a notebook beside your bed to record your dreams. I have seen many people's dream lives increase as a result of doing this. The reason why is because they are stepping out in faith and allowing their expectation that the Lord will speak to them in the night season to increase.

Not Stewarding the Word of the Lord

As we begin hearing the word of God for ourselves, there is often application that comes with hearing. A major key in stewarding the word of the Lord is remembering what the Lord has said. When we position ourselves to steward God's word, we show Him that we value what He says, which will ultimately increase our capacity to hear.

In the Old Testament, when the Lord did something significant or spoke something profound, men and women would often build an altar for the Lord. The reason why they did this was so that everyone who would see these altars would remember what the Lord did or said. It was essentially a way to preserve testimony, and to renew their minds in the goodness and faithfulness of God. Woven within the culture of Israel was an understanding of the importance of remembering what the Lord has done or said.

Journaling can be a profound tool in stewarding the word of the Lord. When we intentionally record our dreams, we prove ourselves as good stewards of God's word, thereby increasing the frequency and consistency of dreams from the Lord. Personally, I have journaled every profound dream that God has given me concerning my calling, in order to remember what the Lord has said. This also gives me the liberty to go back to reread the dreams, so I can begin to reshape the way I view myself based on what God has said about me.

Lack of Proper Positioning

In Job 33:15-16, we can see that it is often in our dreams that the Lord decrees instruction for our lives. Let me ask you a question: Have you ever taken into consideration that your day does not begin when you wake up in the morning? Your day actually begins at 12:00am. Take a look at this verse with me:

In the creation account in Genesis 1:5 it says, "God called the light Day, and the darkness He called Night. So the evening and the morning were the first day." Notice in this verse that the evening is mentioned before the morning, implying that when we go to bed that this is in fact the start of our day.

Unlocking the Language of Dreams

So what does all of this mean? This means that God is laying the foundation of your day while you sleep. As you dream, God is prophesying into your spirit what you will live out when you awake. God uses our evening encounters with Him to sow into our day when we rise.

Ephesians 4:26: "Be angry, and do not sin: do not let the sun go down on your wrath, nor give place to the devil."

It is interesting that we are instructed to not let the sun go down on our wrath. Could the reason be that there is in fact wisdom in positioning ourselves before the Lord with a pure heart before we go to sleep so that we can fully receive what He wants to communicate to us? When I go to sleep at night, I try to make it a priority to position myself in the joy and peace of the Lord. Doing this alone has actually brought an increase in my ability to hear God through dreams.

Matthew 5:8: "Blessed are the pure in heart, for they shall see God."

Receiving from God in the Night Season

When we go to sleep, if we do not allow the joy and peace of God to be established in us, then we actually put up barriers that can prevent us from receiving from God through dreams. It is the same concept of going into a worship gathering, but holding offense in your heart from occurrences that took place earlier in the day. You are there to worship the Lord and connect with His heart, yet there is a disconnect. When you can align your heart by posturing yourself in God's presence while falling asleep, you position yourself to receive from Him throughout the night. You position yourself to allow God to build a proper foundation of the word of the Lord for your day.

Night Terrors

I am sure that some of you reading can recall having night terrors as a child. In fact, this is quite common to experience. Night terrors are not from the Lord. God's heart is not to torment you. In fact, if you have a dream that torments you, you have every right to dismiss it. God's heart is to lavish His love on you through dreams and to give you instruction.

Since the enemy knows that dreams are a common way that God desires to speak to His children, he will try to prevent that from happening, sometimes by using night terrors to make children fear dreams. This often results in children slipping into a survivor mentality regarding their dream lives, subconsciously not permitting themselves to dream in the night.

I was much like this as a child. Due to some in my family who had previously been involved in the occult, I was greatly tormented by the demonic as a child. Much of these attacks would come in the form of dreams. Due to fear, I subconsciously made the decision to stop receiving in my dreams. Even for the first few years after I met the Lord when I was 16 years old, I hardly dreamt. However, as I grew in friendship and intimacy with the Lord, I began to let my guard down in my dream life. God brought profound healing to my heart, which permitted the Lord to commune with me in the night season through dreams.

God's heart is that we will walk in peace in every aspect of our lives. This includes our sleep. For anyone who had night terrors as a child and has experienced a blockage in their dream lives in this way, I believe that it is God's heart to bring full restoration. If this applies to you, then I would invite you to pray this prayer with me:

Receiving from God in the Night Season

"Holy Spirit, I pray that You will give me faith to know that You are my shield of protection in the night. I give to You any fears that I may have surrounding dreams. I pray for peace in the night season. I pray that You would begin to minister to my heart and dismantle any barriers that I may have unknowingly put up, preventing You from speaking to me through the language of dreams. Bring restoration to my dream life. I pray this in the name of Jesus."

Orphan Mentalities

Daniel and Joseph had the most prominent dream interpretation ministries in the Bible. Daniel 1:17 says, "As for these four young men, God gave them knowledge and skill in all literature and wisdom; and Daniel had understanding in all visions and dreams."

This verse says that Daniel could understand and interpret all dreams and visions. Often in scripture we can find a lot of revelation by looking at the meanings of people's names. The name Daniel means, "God is my judge" in Hebrew. Names are a continuous declaration of who we were created to be. I believe that Daniel's revelation of God being his Judge had a key part to play in unlocking his understanding of visions and dreams.

Unlocking the Language of Dreams

The word "judge" in Greek actually means "to distinguish". When we receive God as our Judge in New Testament times, we invite Him to distinguish and bring correction into our lives, thereby allowing Him to refine us. We allow Holy Spirit to distinguish sonship from orphanship within us.

I once had a very interesting vision a while back. I saw God seated on His throne in heavenly splendor. From His throne flowed two rivers over the nations. However, they were not rivers of water; they were rivers of fire. One of the rivers was named, "The Fire of Revival". The other was named, "The Refiner's Fire". The Lord then spoke from His throne saying, "You cannot have one without the other."

The Refiner's fire comes upon the hearts of God's children to burn away the chaff of orphanship, therefore revealing refined sons and daughters. It aligns hearts, so that what God wants to release over the church will be able to be stewarded healthily and orderly.

There is a very key revelation that God is restoring to the church in this day relating to the fear of the Lord and repentance. In fact, repentance is not only pivotal for a true move of the Spirit, but it is essential in order to clearly hear the word of the Lord. This is also true if we want to hear God through dreams. When we do not allow God to lead us to a place where we have a high standard for holy living, we choose to live below the standard of life we were created to live.

Take a look at Holy Spirit's name. His name is not just "Holy"; nor is it just "Spirit". He is Holy Spirit. Within the essence of who He is, He is a place of marriage where holiness and spirit exist as one. He is not one or the other. He is both. His function and purpose is not only to train us to walk in the things of the Spirit, such as the gifts of the Spirit (1 Corinthians 12:8-10), but also in Godly character, as evidenced by the fruits of the Spirit (Galatians 5:22-23).

We can see in the Bible that God is quite passionate about holiness. That being said, I believe it hurts His heart when our standard of holiness is low. I believe that God is raising the bar of holiness again in this time. It is not that God wants to control us, but because He knows that when we live a healthy life, we will be able to experience the fullness of His love. This is why repentance is a prominent part of revival. If we want to walk in a revelation of what the Lord is saying, it is key that we walk in purity of heart.

Before Jesus began His ministry, John the Baptist ministered a message of repentance to Israel and Judah. He was bringing their hearts into alignment so they could experience the fullness of what Jesus had to offer. Once Jesus came on the scene in ministry, He taught repentance as well, saying, "Repent for the kingdom of heaven is at hand" (Matthew 3:2).

Unlocking the Language of Dreams

Repentance happened before revival, and while it was occurring, because God is interested in keeping our hearts in check, so we can experience the full blessing of a move of the Spirit.

Often when we live in sin, we hinder communication with the Godhead. It is not that God is not speaking, because He still is. God is not closed off from us; however, when we live in sin, we close ourselves off from experiencing the fullness of what God has for us.

As we learn to receive God as our Judge and are reformed to re-patterning our minds like sons and daughters instead of orphans, then we can be entrusted with the secrets of God hidden within dreams and visions. A fuller expression of the voice of God opens up to us.

The Vast Array of Dreams

I have learned that dreams are a much deeper topic than I once thought. Not only is the topic deep, but its scope is also vast. It is a shame that the language of dreams is often disregarded by many. Dreams are a powerful tool from the Lord, especially when we begin to understand the varieties of types of dreams that are possible.

In this chapter, I want to walk with you through 14 different types of dreams that I have discovered we can have. Many of the specific terms I have used are not found in scripture; however, they are terms I have come up with to better explain Biblical examples found throughout scripture and that I have experienced in my own life.

Symbolic Dreams

As we are beginning to discern the voice of God in our dreams, it is important for us not to dismiss those things in our dreams that we do not understand. Many of us have a tendency to dismiss our dreams because of their symbolic nature. What we often view as a random ensemble of imagery, can often be a message from the Lord hidden within the symbols. Most dreams are symbolic in nature and require Spirit-directed interpretation.

In the following chapter, you will be trained how to interpret symbols within dreams, so you can understand what God is saying through the symbols of dreams.

Vision of the Night

Job 33:15-16: "In a dream, in a vision of the night, when deep sleep falls upon men, while slumbering on their beds, then He opens the ears of men, and seals

The Vast Array of Dreams

their instruction."

This verse differentiates between dreams and Visions of the Night; two different ways the Lord will speak in the night. Dreams are often filled with symbols, whereas Visions of the Night are more straight forward. Instead of consisting of symbolic imagery, visions are plain and do not require interpretation.

In Acts 2:18, it says that when Holy Spirit pours out that "your young men shall see visions, your old men shall dream dreams." This shows us that knowing the voice of the Lord through dreams is actually a mark of maturity. This is because dreams consist of symbols and require interpretation, whereas visions are more straight forward.

Let's look at the following scriptures relating to Visions of the Night:

Acts 16:9: "A vision appeared to Paul in the night. A man of Macedonia stood and pleaded with him, saying, 'Come over to Macedonia and help us.'"

Acts 18:9-10: "Now the Lord spoke to Paul in the night by a vision, 'Do not be afraid, but speak, and do not keep silent; for I am with you, and no one will attack you to hurt you; for I have many people in this city.' And he continued *there* a year and six months, teaching the word of God among them."

I had a Vision of the Night a while back about a good friend of mine who is in business. In this Vision of the Night, I saw him sitting around a table with a group of business leaders. He was teaching and training them how to make millions of dollars for the kingdom of God. It was a very powerful, yet simple Vision of the Night.

When I brought this Vision of the Night that I had to my friend, he was shocked. He told me that only a few days before, he was telling his wife that God placed a new dream in his heart, which was to train business leaders in how to make millions of dollars for the kingdom of heaven. It was only a few months later when he began finding himself in business meetings where he was influencing business leaders who were millionaires.

Trance

Acts 11:5: *"I was in the city of Joppa praying, and in a trance I saw a vision, an object descending like a great sheet, let down from heaven by four corners; and it came to me."*

The Vast Array of Dreams

A trance is not necessarily a dream, however, it could fit in with the dream category to some degree. The word "trance" may sound like something used in New Age practices, but scripture shows that this is a way that God speaks today. The enemy does not have the ability to create, but he will try to steal what God has already created and try and pervert it. It is time that we claim back and redeem what God has created for His children.

The word "trance" translated into Greek is "extasis", which is from the word "existemi", which literally means "ecstasy". The definition of ecstasy is: "displacing the individual's state of mind with an elevated God given state for the purpose of instructing him."

In Acts 11:5, it says that when Peter was in a trance, he saw a vision. A trance is a state of raised awareness that we can fall into so that we can clearly hear what Holy Spirit is speaking to us. Trances are actually a very common thing, which you may have already experienced without even realizing it. I am just going to add terminology and show you the significance to spiritual experiences which are often overlooked. Do you know that feeling when you are in between wakefulness and asleep? Your mind starts showing you things that you would never have thought of when you were awake. Not every time, but I believe that a lot of the time, this is a trance.

Here is another example of a trance: While you have been worshipping, have you ever felt so consumed with the Lord's presence that you could not take your focus from Him even if you tried? If so, then you have experienced a trance. In these moments, you are in an enhanced awareness of what God is doing and saying. This is a trance from the Lord.

God speaks through things like dreams, visions and trances because they bypass our intellect and logic so that we do not reason ourselves out of hearing God's word.

Numbers 24:4,16: *"he hath said, which heard the words of God, which saw the vision of the Almighty, falling into a trance, but having his eyes open..."* (KJV)

Demonic Dream

John 10:10: "The thief does not come except to steal, and to kill, and to destroy."

We have discussed how it is not likely that every dream we have is from God. Although dreams are a common avenue that God uses to speak truth to us, it is also something the enemy will try to use to speak

The Vast Array of Dreams

lies. Dreams are from the Lord, however, the enemy wants to pervert this avenue so we are not utilizing every facet that the Lord can use to speak to us.

A good way to tell if a dream is from the enemy, is to ask yourself if the dream was tormenting at all to you. If a dream torments you, then you have every right to dismiss it. I have met many people who try to interpret and make sense of dreams from the enemy, but they end up running down a long winding road of confusion. The enemy's goal in trying to speak to you is to lead you into bondage. Therefore, do not give any attention to what he says. Instead, focus on the word of the Lord, so that you can stand in the fullness of His love and freedom.

A helpful way to determine if your dreams are from God or the enemy, is that dreams from the enemy will at times consist of darker or more muted colours. Whereas dreams from God will often be more vibrant. While this can be true at times, God can speak however He chooses, so therefore there are dreams where this may not apply.

Something you can do when you have a demonic dream, is what I like to call "Shifting a Dream". Many years ago, I used to have demonic dreams concerning finances. These dreams would consist of losing my wallet, going into debt, or losing my home. These were clearly not dreams from the Lord. The enemy was targeting this area in my life because there was a mentality of poverty I struggled with at the time.

Since then, thankfully, the Lord has brought me into freedom in this area of my life.

When we are Shifting a Dream, we are recognizing and pinpointing the specific area that the enemy is trying to strike fear into us. In this case, the area that the enemy was attacking was my finances. Since the enemy was narrowing in on this area of my life, I knew that this was an area that the Lord was in fact wanting to bring a change concerning my mentality around provision.

Often when the enemy overplays his hand, he reveals what the Lord actually wants to do in us. Knowing this allowed me to begin declaring the opposite of what the enemy was speaking. The enemy was speaking lies that I would go into debt, but in my intercession I would declare what the Lord was saying. I would declare that I was going to step into the provision of the Lord and that I would walk in peace concerning finances. This is a way how we God redeem a Demonic Dream.

Split Dream

As we are learning about the language of God through dreams, it is important to remember that there is a spiritual battle taking place around us. That being said, there may be times when the Lord is

The Vast Array of Dreams

speaking to you through a dream and the enemy is trying to thwart the word of the Lord, or muffle it, so you do not receive God's message through it.

Have you ever had a dream where certain aspects have the authority of God written all over it, yet other parts bring torment or fear? This is a Split Dream. It is when the Lord speaks through a dream, but the enemy tries to interject and prevent you from receiving the message.

When we have a Split Dream, our job is to discern what is from the Lord and what is not. Once we know what is from the Lord, we can begin to ask Holy Spirit to bring an interpretation for those specific parts. When we see the part that was the enemy's attempt to interject, we can then dismiss that part of the dream. It is not our job to try to discern the enemy's voice, so I would advise you to simply dismiss whatever the enemy may be trying to communicate.

Soul Dream

A Soul Dream occurs when there is not necessarily any spiritual influence guiding our dreams, but instead, it is our imagination creating the imagery we are seeing. Sometimes in these dreams, we will be processing our day or circumstances in the realm of the mind, emotions and imagination. Although this dream type does not seem overly interesting, it does benefit us to know that this is a type of dream. I have met many people who spend much time trying to interpret these types of dreams believing that they are God, when really, it is their soul processing the occurrences of their life. These dreams are actually a gift that God has given to help us process our lives.

Inner Healing Dream

I have a friend who a few years ago, had a dream from the Lord that brought profound healing to her heart.

In the dream she was in the ocean, and knew that there were sharks swimming all around her. This caused her to greatly fear for her life in this dream. She had experienced much tragedy at a younger age and during the time the dream occurred she had a very strong fear of death. There was trauma surrounding death in her heart.

As the dream progressed, she saw an angel walking on the water, who invited her to walk on the water with it. My friend, was then no longer swimming with the sharks, but walking on the water with the angel. At this point, the fear no longer existed in her heart.

Since it is never God's heart to torment us, I used to think that if we experienced strong fear, anxiety or insecurity in a dream that the dream was not from God. Now, after having much more experience with dream interpretation, I have learned that while it is true that God will never torment us, He will at times use a dream to surface fear, anxiety or insecurity that may already exist in our hearts for the purpose of bringing healing and freedom. This is what an Inner Healing Dream is.

My friend experienced tremendous healing in her heart through this dream, which initiated a journey where she began to fully step out of the trauma that was in her life surrounding death.

As we embrace the voice of God through dreams, God could very well use what He says in the night season to bring healing to pain and wounding within our soul.

Encounter Dream

There are certain dreams where it is as though we are watching a movie unfold before our eyes. There are other dreams where we are in control of what is taking place. Even though we are dreaming, in these types of dreams we are in control of our actions, thoughts and emotions. This is an Encounter Dream.

The Bible tells us that angels and demons are real. Heaven is real. The tangibility of God is real. What God's word shares with us about the spirit realm is not a fairy tale, nor should it be treated as such. We are in a constant state of interacting with what occurs in the realm of the spirit, often without us even realizing it. Consequently, there are also times in our dreams when we are interacting with things that are occurring around us in the spirit.

I once had a dream where I was in a library. In this dream, I was in complete control of my actions, thoughts and emotions. As I walked through this library, there was an angel that guided me to a specific table. Upon the table sat a small treasure chest. As I opened the chest, I saw a small key inside of it. I picked up the key and felt the weight of it. It was unexpectedly heavy. The Lord then began to speak to me in the dream, telling me that this key was symbolic of a specific spiritual gift that He had ordained for me to walk in. He then began to speak to me about the cost that I would have to pay to walk in such a gifting. He spoke to me specifically, explaining that walking in this gifting would result in many lives being impacted; however, because of the nature of the gifting, it would also cause some to misunderstand me. After giving me clear instruction concerning this gifting, the Lord then gave me the choice as to whether or not I would take the key. I was given a decision to either pick up this spiritual gift that God had ordained for me, or to leave it. In the dream, I decided to take the key, to embrace the greater things that the Lord has called me to.

In this dream, not only was I in control of what I was doing, but I actually made a pivotal decision to pay the required cost to walk in the greater things that God has ordained for my life. This was more than just a dream where God was communicating something through symbols. This was an encounter that is still having an impact on my life to this day.

Heavenly Dream

Ephesians 1:3: "Blessed be the God and Father of our Lord Jesus Christ, who has blessed us with every spiritual blessing in the heavenly places in Christ."

A Heavenly Dream occurs when we see and experience heaven while we sleep. This type of dream may look like a scenario unfolding before our eyes, or it could be more like an Encounter Dream where we are in control of ourselves in the dream. The Bible is filled with stories of men and women of God who have had heavenly experiences. Ephesians 2:6 talks about how we are actually seated in heavenly places, in Christ. The goodness of the kingdom of heaven is our

Unlocking the Language of Dreams

constant reality as believers, and through the cross we have access to experience every spiritual blessing in heavenly places.

Here are a few Biblical references for you to look at on your own time to build your faith relating to heavenly encounters:

- Ezekiel 1
- Revelation 4
- 2 Corinthians 12:1-3
- Isaiah 6
- Daniel 7:9-10
- Genesis 28:12-22

If you are interested in learning about heavenly dreams and encounters, I encourage you to read my book "A Timeless Journey". It is a compilation of numerous dreams, visions and encounters I have had about heaven.

The Vast Array of Dreams

Intercession Dream

I have met many intercessors who, through their dreams, receive insight into how God wants them to pray.

A while back I had a very interesting dream about a particular city. In this dream, I was looking at the city from an aerial perspective. Over the city were four demonic rulers in the sky in the shape of funnel clouds. About one week later, as I was driving with the Lord, He began to speak to me about how a tornado was going to hit this city that I saw in my dream.

Now, this was an odd word to receive, considering that this city does not have a history of tornadoes. There was one tornado, which the Lord had also given me prior notice of, that had hit the city a few years earlier. However, other than that, there had not been a tornado in this city since the 1970's. The Lord went on to share with me that this coming tornado was an outward expression of the spiritual warfare that was occurring in the city at the time, and that the Lord was calling the church to intercession and prayer.

To my surprise, the very next day, a small tornado hit this city. Thankfully, no one was harmed. Not only did a tornado hit the city, but on that same day there were also four other funnel clouds sighted, just as in my dream. Spending much of that day in prayer for this city, I then went on to contact various intercessors and pastors throughout the city, giving them prophetic insight and strategy as to how to pray. This resulted in a great spiritual shift in the city. It was through a dream that the Lord gave direction concerning how the intercessors needed to pray.

I have met different intercessors and prophetic leaders where God does not only give them insight in how they should pray through their dreams. They have had times where they come into a state of intercession and prayer within their dreams, advancing God's kingdom even while they are asleep.

This might seem strange to some, however look at the following scripture:

1 Corinthians 2:10: "God has revealed them to us through His Spirit. For the Spirit searches all things, yes, the deep things of God. For what man knows the things of a man except the spirit of a man which is in him? Even so no one knows the things of God except the Spirit of God. Now we have received, not the spirit of the world, but the Spirit who is from God, that we might know the things that have been freely given to us by God."

When we first receive Holy Spirit, He merges with our spirit and we become one spirit with Him (1 Corinthians 6:17). Holy Spirit walks in perfect relationship with the Father and the Son. Since He is constantly in fellowship with them, He is continually searching out the deep things of God. Our spirits are one with Him, meaning that our spirits can constantly keep in step with Holy Spirit while He is searching out the deep secrets of God's heart. It is comforting to know that there is a part in all of us that is never willing to stop pushing to know the full magnitude of who God is. Revelation 4 talks about the four living creatures who worship the Lord day and night. They are able to operate without the need for sleep because they are spiritual beings and therefore do not require physical rest. An exciting truth is that all night long while our bodies are sleeping, our spirits are hungrily awake, interacting with God and constantly receiving from Him.

I have met many intercessors and prophetic people who will pray over people in their dreams, or will be in a state of intercession for specific cities, regions or people groups. We can never allow ourselves to try to limit God with our finite belief of what is possible. God can move however He chooses to move. We need to be in a place to allow God to use us no matter how He chooses to do so.

End-Time Dreams

John 16:13: "When the Spirit of truth comes, he will guide you into all truth. He will not speak on his own but will tell you what he has heard. He will tell you about the future."

Often when God gives us dreams, it is often to speak to us regarding our own lives. He can also give us dreams concerning others. However, I have met many prophetic leaders who have had the Lord speak to them concerning the end-times through their dreams. Although these dreams seem to be rarer, there are a variety of reasons why God might bring awareness to such things. God could share these things to call the church to co-labour with Him to intercede for what is to take place in the future. Another reason could be to show the church how they should position themselves for what is to come. God could also be sharing this with someone simply because He desires to share with His people what is on His heart (Amos 3:7).

Daniel is an excellent Biblical example of someone who had End-Time Dreams. We can see in scripture that Daniel was given insight as to what was occurring in his present time. However, there were also times when Daniel was given insight to what would occur years after he was no longer alive *(Daniel 7)*.

The Vast Array of Dreams

If you receive End-Time Dreams, I would encourage you to ask Holy Spirit for insight into their meanings. I have met many who thought that they had a dream about the end times, when they actually had a symbolic dream and thought it was literal. As you seek Holy Spirit for understanding and instruction, He will reveal what to do with such dreams. Whether it is taking a posture of Spirit-led intercession, journaling what the Lord is saying, communicating the dream with others, or any other way God may lead you, it is important to remember that Holy Spirit is worthy to be trusted in His leading.

Warning Dream

God will often give us dreams to warn us of the enemy's schemes, or to prepare us for circumstances that are coming our way. If we think of a Warning Dream, we may feel a level of anxiety around it as warnings often have a negative connotation to it. However, it is important to understand that God warns us out of His kindness so that we can live in the fullness of His promises. Warning Dreams give us insight into how to position ourselves properly to align ourselves with God's will. Warning Dreams could also give us insight into how to pray so that we can side-step the enemy's plans toward us.

Unlocking the Language of Dreams

In medieval time periods, men were stationed upon city walls to watch for the enemy. They would stand watch to discern the enemy's strategy. God wants to raise us up as watchmen and watchwomen on the wall so that we may understand the enemy's strategy and how to stand in authority, while at the same time resting in the peace of God.

When God gives us a Warning Dream, He is making us aware of the enemy's tactics towards us. He is guiding us, so we can position ourselves in the promises of God, even though there may be a form of strategic opposition coming.

There are two different ways God can expose the enemy's schemes in a Warning Dream. He could either warn us of upcoming circumstances, or He could warn us of the enemy's schemes in our lives relating to unchecked sin, or unhealthy habits and mindsets that we are walking in. In a Warning Dream, God could expose something occurring in our hearts that could be detrimental to us. It is God's kindness when He exposes unhealthy sin, habits or mindsets, so we can walk in the fullness of what God has for us.

John 16:17-18: "Nevertheless I tell you the truth. It is to your advantage that I go away; for if I do not go away, the Helper (Holy Spirit) will not come to you; but if I depart, I will send Him to you. And when He has come, He will convict the world of sin, and of righteousness, and of judgment."

The Vast Array of Dreams

We really need to pay attention when Holy Spirit speaks to us through dreams, warning us of the enemy's schemes against upcoming events and situations.

God gave me a dream shortly before He began expanding my and my wife's ministry. In the dream, my wife and I were invited to an exclusive club at someone's home for those who were in high levels of leadership in the church. As we arrived, we began to feel very uncomfortable, as it felt as though the people we conversed with had a mentality of elitism. Everyone at the party was going around flattering one another in order to be viewed as important. We felt very uncomfortable and decided to leave the gathering.

Once I woke up, the Lord began to speak to me through the dream, explaining that when promoted into high levels of influence, there is a temptation to slip into an elitist mentality and the key to avoiding this is to intentionally posture yourself in humility. Humility is the greatest weapon against a mentality of elitism.

God used this dream to warn me of the potential threat of adopting an elitist mentality as He was promoting us into greater influence. This dream helped remind me to intentionally walk in a posture of humility and showed me that humility is one of the great keys to walking out your calling with longevity.

Unlocking the Language of Dreams

When God gives us warnings, He does it because He cares about keeping us in accordance with His will. As a Friend, He guides us, bringing clarity to our path, that we may experience the fullness of the adventure that He has set before us.

Direction Dream

A Direction Dream is when the Lord gives us clear direction in life, much like the testimony that I shared in the opening chapter of this book.

An example of a Direction Dream in scripture was when God spoke to Pharaoh in the night season in Genesis 41:1-7. Since Pharaoh did not know the interpretation of the symbols in his dreams, he consulted with Joseph. Joseph told Pharaoh that the Lord was communicating that there would be seven years of plenty, which would follow seven years of famine. These dreams actually gave Pharaoh instruction in how he should lead his kingdom. It gave him direction to store food in preparation for what was to come.

If you are unsure of the direction that you feel you are receiving in a dream, I would encourage you to run your dream and interpretation by someone you trust who hears the Lord. There is much wisdom in

The Vast Array of Dreams

positioning yourself to receive counsel from those who know the Lord intimately. For myself, I have a team of people who I am in covenant relationship with. When I feel like the Lord is bringing a drastic shift in my direction in life, I consult with those who know my heart. Your covenant relationships are one of your greatest keys in keeping on track with the calling over your life.

Proverbs 15:22: "Without counsel, plans go awry, but in the multitude of counsellors they are established."

Calling Dream

A Calling Dream is when the Lord speaks to you in a dream about the calling and destiny over your life. Joseph had a very profound calling dream in Genesis 37:7-8, when the Lord showed him his call as a leader to rule and reign. This was a specific dream about his purpose in who God had created him to be.

God speaks Calling Dreams to affirm us in the unique calling over our lives. It is very essential for us to learn to remember the word of the Lord, especially in Calling Dreams. Joseph held onto his dream for over 20 years and it finally came to pass. Joseph needed not only to remember the word of the Lord, but he needed to continually renew his mind in the promise that he was given through his dream. I believe that the promise he received through his dream is actually what helped sustain him through his time of trials.

I have had many dreams where the Lord has spoken to me about the calling over my life. I have found it very beneficial to record those dreams. Often, if I am in a time where I slip into self-doubt, I find it beneficial to go back and read those dreams. I renew my mind in what the Lord has declared over me. God's word is not something that we should hear and then forget. God's word is something that we should hear, and then pull into our heart. God's word is not a quick fix for insecurity. It is precious, and if stewarded properly, it will be able to sustain you until you step into the fullness of its complete expression.

There may be times when no one will be able to see the calling and destiny over your life except you. In these times we need to remember what the Lord has said. Renewing your mind in the prophetic destiny that God has spoken over your life will teach you to stand when everyone expects you to sit. The same can be said for dreams. As God speaks into us in the night season, we need to hold His word in our heart.

The Vast Array of Dreams

Impartation

As you were reading through this list of different types of dreams, I am sure that you recognized a few from your own dream life. Others may have been new or foreign to you. Either way, I believe that there is an opportunity right now for increase. As I had previously mentioned, sometimes we can experience an increase in the ways of God simply by learning that it is possible. My heart is that you will be able to hear God in whichever way He chooses to speak to you. For some, God may open up your dreams to experience all of His diverse ways. For others, God may narrow in on a specific dream to begin to teach you about it. God may also begin to journey with you to broaden His language towards you in a different way entirely. However, if you would like to receive an impartation from the Lord to experience an increase in the different ways that God speaks through dreams, then pray this prayer with me by faith:

"Holy Spirit, broaden my capacity to hear Your voice through dreams. I pray that You would begin to reveal Yourself to me however You desire. I ask for discernment to know when it is You speaking, and when it is not. Fine tune my ears to hear Your voice in all ways. Speak to me as a friend speaks to a friend."

Interpreting Symbols

Genesis 37:5-8: "Now Joseph had a dream, and he told it to his brothers; and they hated him even more. So he said to them, 'Please hear this dream which I have dreamed: There we were, binding sheaves in the field. Then behold, my sheaf arose and also stood upright; and indeed your sheaves stood all around and bowed down to my sheaf.' And his brothers said to him, 'Shall you indeed reign over us? Or shall you indeed have dominion over us?' So they hated him even more for his dreams and for his words."

In order for us to understand the language of dreams, we need to come into an understanding of

Unlocking the Language of Dreams

how God uses symbols to communicate. There is something very intriguing to me in this passage with Joseph and his brothers. We can see that Joseph had a dream that was filled with symbolism. However, the fascinating thing is that when he shared the dream with his brothers, he did not interpret it for them. His brothers knew exactly what it meant. What this tells me is that in their time period, people were learned in the language of dreams.

It is amazing how many dreams we dismiss, simply because we do not understand how to interpret their symbols. We brush off our dreams as random and nonsensical, when really, buried within the mystery of the symbols, is a message from the heart of God for us. This was the same approach that Jesus took in the gospels. We can see in scripture that Jesus spoke in symbols on numerous occasions. There were times when He spoke plainly; however, He would often teach in parables and symbols (Matthew 13:34).

Jesus spoke to the masses in parables. He used stories as a tool to spark the imagination, to teach and to communicate truth. The amazing thing is that these parables often left people confused because He did not speak plainly to them. He did this to hide truth from the proud, because it is only the humble and the hungry who will search through the riddles and symbols to find the word of the Lord. The same can be said for dreams. In dreams, the Lord often speaks in mysteries and in parables, knowing that only those who are truly hungry for truth will search for the

Interpreting Symbols

message hidden within the symbols.

The best advice that I could ever give relating to dream interpretation is that we should never try to interpret our dreams apart from Holy Spirit. He is the key to understanding dreams.

Genesis 40:8: "And they said to him (Joseph), 'We each have had a dream, and there is no interpreter of it.' So Joseph said to them, 'Do not interpretations belong to God? Tell them to me, please.'"

1 Corinthians 2:10: "The Spirit searches all things, yes, the deep things of God."

As soon as we begin trying to interpret dreams based on our own logic or system, we end up getting fleshly interpretations. We do not want interpretations that are fleshly. We need interpretations of the Spirit.

We cannot depend on our logic for interpretation because God communicates to each of us differently and not all symbols will mean the same thing to every individual. If symbols always meant the same thing, it would not be difficult to make a computer program where you simply type in your dream to receive an interpretation.

Unlocking the Language of Dreams

For example, when I have a dream about a horse, it is often symbolic of power, authority, or a move of the Spirit. However, if someone grew up on a farm around horses, having a dream of a horse could mean something completely different to them. To them, a horse might be symbolic of safety, belonging or home. God's relationship with each of us is drastically unique so the way He uses symbols to speak to each of us may be very different. I know of different prophetic leaders whose teachings about the meanings of symbols are in great contrast. It is not that any are necessarily wrong in their interpretations, but that God speaks in diverse ways to His children. As you look at the dream dictionary at the back of this book, you will notice that there are numerous interpretations for most of the symbols. It is likely that there are even more interpretations than what is included there.

What I want to do right now to teach you how to properly interpret a dream, is to give you a few examples of dreams and show you the approach I use to receive the interpretation.

Interpreting Symbols

Dream #1:

One of my friends shared the following dream with me: In this dream, she was in a building where a party was taking place with many people whom she recognized from church. As she was conversing with others, she saw something in her peripheral vision. It was a snake slithering on the ground. In the dream, this snake slithered over to a woman and up her body. Once the snake reached her head, it bit her. My friend and two other women walked up to this woman and prayed over her, which resulted in the healing of the wound.

Suddenly, the dream changed and she found herself in the basement of the same building. The main thing that stuck out to her in the basement was a table with a large sword laying upon it.

These are the types of dreams that we often dismiss because they are full of symbolism and not literal. However, God hides treasures of revelation within parables and symbols. Take a look at how we can interpret this dream:

Interpretation of Dream #1

As we are interpreting dreams, we need to pay attention to the details. The first thing that we notice about this dream is that it takes place in a building.

When someone has a dream about a house, it is often symbolic of the dreamer's life. However, buildings are usually symbolic of the church, or the kingdom of heaven. Buildings can also be symbolic of someone's career or ministry. The fact that the dreamer was seeing many people from church in the building confirms that it was referring to the church.

The next thing we see is that the dreamer sees a snake slithering on the ground. When we are interpreting a symbol, we can look for that specific symbol to see if it is in scripture. If it is in scripture, then this may give us some insight into what the interpretation is. Whether that specific symbol is in scripture or not, we need to be listening to Holy Spirit to hear if He is giving us insight to what it could mean. Looking at the characteristics of the symbol could also give us insight into its meaning.

In this case, we know that snakes are mentioned in the Bible, and they usually refer to the enemy (Genesis 3:1). Snakes can also be symbolic of deception and lies.

We see that in the next part of this dream, the serpent bites a woman on the head. Remember, we

Interpreting Symbols

need to pay attention to the details. The serpent did not bite the woman's ankle or hand. It bit her head and there is meaning behind that fact. Heads are often symbolic of an authority figure, just as Jesus is referred to as the Head of the church (Colossians 1:18). Heads could also be symbolic of a specific mindset. In this case, while asking Holy Spirit, I felt like He said that the head in this dream was symbolic of a teaching anointing in the church, as teachers often train and equip the body of Christ in the realm of the mind. After this takes place, we see that my friend and two others go to pray with the woman and her wound is healed.

Then the dream suddenly shifts and she is in the basement. Now, when we have a dream about a house or a building, we need to pay attention to where we are inside that building because different rooms mean different things. If you are dreaming about a bedroom, it could be symbolic of your intimacy with the Lord, or of your marriage. If you dream about a kitchen, it could be symbolic of your spiritual nourishment or about a time of preparation. If you dream about an attic, it would likely symbolize history or your memories. Basements are often symbolic of the soul, as it is the deep of the deep in a house.

The dreamer looks around and sees a table with a sword laying upon it. Remember that scripture can help us with interpretation. Swords in the Bible often symbolize the Word of God (Ephesians 6:17).

Unlocking the Language of Dreams

Now that we understand what the symbols mean in this dream, let's look at what the message of God would be in context with the dream:

I believe that this dream was about how there has been an attack of the enemy toward the church to try to wound the teacher anointing within the body of Christ. The enemy has attacked it with deception and lies. However, God is raising up this dreamer to confront this wound so that it can be healed, thereby restoring this area of ministry again to the church. The fact that the dream shifted to the basement tells us that the dreamer's effectiveness in this is not only to impact surface levels in the church. It will penetrate the heart and soul of the church because she will be wielding the sword of the Spirit, the Word of God.

It is amazing how, at first glance, this dream seemed like a jumble of random occurrences. Yet, when we understand the language of God, there is a clear message from the heart of the Lord. As you saw in this interpretation, there are three questions we can ask ourselves while trying to decipher symbols:

- What is Holy Spirit saying about what this symbol could symbolize?

- Is this symbol in scripture? If so, does this give me insight to what the Lord might be saying?

Interpreting Symbols

- Do the characteristics of this symbol give me any insight to its meaning?

Dream #2

A friend of mine had a dream where she was outside, in the backyard of a house where she grew up. In the backyard, the ground was covered in wintery snow. As she watched the snow, she saw a black rabbit dash across the snowy floor. Suddenly, she saw something out of the corner of her eye. Perched upon a tree branch were seven crows who had all frozen to death. All seven crows then fell out of the tree.

Interpretation #2

The first thing that we want to take notice of in this dream is the significance of the fact that it took place in the dreamer's backyard, where she grew up. This tells me that this dream is not only referring to her current season, but that there is an overarching message here regarding her life.

Unlocking the Language of Dreams

One of the first symbols that we notice in this dream is the snow. Snow can be symbolic of a variety of different things; however, in this dream, it was symbolic of purity. This speaks to how this dreamer has had a pure heart to know the Lord since she was a little girl. The black rabbit is symbolic of the dreamer and how she has grown at an accelerated pace with the Lord. This would be an analogy speaking to the fact that she has felt very set apart throughout her life, almost as though she were a "black sheep" in her circles, because of her unique relationship with the Lord.

Crows are rarely good in dreams, and often symbolize demonic opposition or demonic assignment. This would speak to how the dreamer has felt a form of opposition toward her calling, and that there have been specific things that she has been contending for in her life. The fact that seven crows froze to death is very significant. Seven is usually the number of completion since the earth was completed in creation throughout the span of seven days. This is actually God declaring that the season of opposition is coming to a close for the dreamer, and that a new season will be beginning. It is a time of breakthrough, saying that the things that may have hindered her in the past, will not hinder her anymore. The fact that the snow and cold temperature is what killed the crows, speaks to how her pure heart for the Lord has prevented the enemy from having a foothold in her life, which stopped the plan of the enemy from having any effect.

Interpreting Symbols

Symbols, Colours, Numbers, People and Emotions

Often while I am interpreting dreams, I will ask myself these five questions:

- What are the main symbols?

- Are there any colours that stick out in the dream?

- Are there any significant numbers in the dream?

- Who are the main people in this dream?

- Were there any primary emotions that stuck out in the dream?

These five questions can begin to unlock to us key revelation that God may be wanting to communicate through dreams. You will notice in the second dream interpretation we just walked through, that understanding what God was saying through colours and numbers was crucial in what He was communicating. In the Dream Dictionary section of this book, I have explained some things God might communicate through different symbols, colours, numbers, people and emotions.

Impartation

I hope that this chapter gave insight into how you can interpret your dreams with the Lord. I would encourage you to go through some dreams that you have had in the past and walk through the dream interpretation steps. Always remember to invite Holy Spirit to shine clarity as you are believing for an interpretation. If you would like an increase in your ability to understand symbols in your dreams, then pray the following prayer in faith with me.

"Holy Spirit, I pray for an increase to understand Your language through symbols and parables. Help me to partner with You, so that I can have a full revelation of what You are speaking in the night season. I pray for gifts of interpretation, that I will have clarity in my own dream life, as well as understanding to help others who do not understand their own dreams."

Dream Interpretation Dictionary

Common Questions About Dreams

Are all dreams from God?

Not all dreams are from God. There are three sources where we can receive dreams from. We can receive dreams from God, from the enemy, or from our own soul.

Do symbols always mean the same thing?

Symbols, colours and numbers do not definitively mean one thing in dreams. Since we are all created with a unique relationship with the Lord, symbols might mean one thing to one person, yet another thing to someone else. Dream interpretation is not a systematic endeavor. It is actually impossible to correctly interpret dreams apart from Holy Spirit's guidance.

Why do I have trouble interpreting my own dreams?

I have met many people who are gifted in interpreting other people's dreams, yet struggle with interpreting their own. There are a few reasons why this may occur. The first is that the dreamer is emotionally connected with their life. Emotion can often cloud discernment. This means that there might be a struggle in interpreting your own dreams, considering that you are so emotionally invested in yourself. This is a very common thing to experience.

Another reason why someone may have troubles interpreting their own dreams is because God wants them to have a healthy dependency on the church. I have met many prophetic leaders who have profound revelation concerning dreams, yet cannot interpret the simplest of their own dreams. Often the reason is because God wants to speak to them through those who they are in relationship with.

Why do I have trouble interpreting my spouse's dreams?

The reason why someone may have trouble interpreting their spouse's dreams is similar to why they may have troubles interpreting their own. You are directly attached to what is occurring in your spouse's life, so therefore the interpretation will directly affect you. This means that your emotion could cloud your discernment while interpreting. That being said, it is still possible to learn to interpret both your own and your spouse's dreams.

What does it mean when you dream in dark or light colours?

A helpful way to determine if your dreams are from God or the enemy, is that dreams from the enemy will at times consist of darker or more muted colours. Whereas dreams from God will often be more vibrant. While this can be true at times, God can speak however He chooses, so therefore there are dreams where this may not apply.

What does it mean when no one can interpret my dream?

Sometimes we can have a dream that not only carries a message for a season, but carries a message for your life. This means that God wants to unfold the interpretation to you through a certain period of time instead of giving you a quick interpretation. When this is the case, God will often veil the meaning from others so that He can reveal the meaning to you how He desires to.

I once had a dream about my calling that was probably one of the most significant dreams I have ever had in my life. I asked many people who were gifted in dream interpretation, yet no one could give me a correct interpretation because it was veiled to them. I held onto that dream for eight years before the Lord unfolded the correct interpretation to me.

What does it mean when I have a reoccurring dream?

Often when we experience this form of consistency with a dream, the Lord is trying to reiterate the importance of the dream. He is prophesying into the dreamer that He wants them to pay close attention to the message hidden within the dream.

The Five Pillars of Dream Interpretation

Based on my experience with dream interpretation, I have found that there are five pillars that we need to pay attention to in order to extract God's messages through dreams. I call them "The Five Pillars of Dream Interpretation". These five pillars are:

- Colours
- Numbers
- People
- Emotions
- Symbols

Understanding how the Lord can speak through all five, can be crucial if we want to understand what God may be communicating in the night season. I am going to walk you through each five to understand what different colours, numbers, people, emotions and symbols could mean in dreams.

It is very important to note that even though I am giving examples of what different colours, numbers or symbols could mean, that these may not be true for every person or dream. We cannot remove Holy Spirit from the process of dream interpretation by depending upon systems. Therefore, this dream dictionary cannot be used to definitively tell you what your dreams mean, but is instead a tool to help you as you are discerning the voice of the Lord.

Colours

Colours are very important to pay attention to when we are interpreting dreams. With colours throughout dreams, different colours could be symbolic of something positive, as well as something negative. Here is a list of some colours and their possible meaning:

White (Positive side): God. Purity. Clarity. Goodness. Faithfulness.

White (Negative side): Religious spirit.

Black (Positive side): Mysteries of God.

Black (Negative side): Bondage. Spiritual warfare. Deception. Demonic stronghold.

Red (Positive side): Power. Authority. The blood of Jesus, Mercy. The apostolic ministry.

Red (Negative side): Anxiety. Pride. Aggression.

Blue (Positive side): Revelation. Wisdom. Holy Spirit. The prophetic ministry.

Unlocking the Language of Dreams

Blue (Negative side): Depression. Sadness. Confusion.

Yellow (Positive side): Childlikeness. Faith. Courage. Bravery. Hope. Knowledge. The ministry of teaching.

Yellow (Negative side): Cowardice. Doubt. Passivity.

Orange (Positive side): Vision. Celebration. Harvest. Evangelism.

Orange (Negative side): Lack of maturity. Witchcraft.

Green: Growth. New life. Creativity. Promise. The pastoral ministry.

Purple: Royalty. Identity.

Brown: Maturity. Humility. Meekness.

Silver: Redemption. Restoration. Finances.

Gold: Refinement. Godly character. Finances. Wealth.

Numbers

Numbers are often very prominent in dreams. Different numbers can mean different things and can be very crucial in understanding God's message through dreams. Here is a list of some numbers and their possible meaning:

1: God. Unity. New beginnings. Isolation. Loneliness.

2: Union. Partnership. Division.

3: The Trinity. Body, soul and spirit.

4: Wholeness. Refining. Creation. Creativity.

5: Grace. The five-fold ministry (Ephesians 4:11-12).

6: A season of life coming to a close. Mankind. Sin.

7: Completion (Genesis 2:2). Rest (Genesis 2:2).

8: New beginnings.

9: Movement of the Spirit. Gifts of the Spirit (1 Corinthians 12:8-10). Fruits of the Spirit (Galatians 5:22-23).

10: Divine order. Judgement. Old Testament. The law. Responsibility.

Unlocking the Language of Dreams

11: Transition. Disorder. Prophet.

12: Government. Apostle.

13: Love (1 Corinthians 13). Rebellion. Witchcraft. Evangelist. Harvest.

14: Double portion. Deliverance. Pastor.

15: Knowledge. Teacher.

16: Established new beginnings.

30: Calling. Destiny.

40: Wilderness. Testing. Trials. Discipline of the Lord.

111 or 1111: Changing seasons. Transition. Stepping into promise (Deuteronomy 11:11).

222 or 2222: The key of David. Doors opening. Doors closing (Isaiah 22:22).

333 or 3333: The mysteries of God. Wisdom. Revelation (Jeremiah 33:3)

123 or 1234: Alignment.

People

    A key in dream interpretation is understanding how God uses people as symbols. One of the greatest stumbling blocks in understanding dreams is that we will often think that when we have a dream with someone in it, that the dream is literally about them. Now, this may be true. It could literally be referring to the person you see in your dream. However, that person could also be a symbol for something else entirely.

    When we are having a dream of a specific person, I have learned two ways that God will often use them as a symbol. The first way is through understanding the meaning of someone's name. Our name is a continuous declaration of who God has created us to be. Sometimes when God shows us someone in our dreams, there is a message hidden within the meaning of their name.

    Here is an example for you: If you are having a dream about someone you know whose name is William, this might not literally be about this specific person. The name William means "protector". God could actually be using William as a symbol to show you that God wants to increase your revelation in knowing that God is your Protector.

Unlocking the Language of Dreams

The second way that God will use people as symbols in dreams, is by what that person could represent to you. This could happen with both the positive and negative attributes of people. For myself, whenever I have a dream with a friend of mine who is an established business leader, God uses him as a symbol of wealth. Every time I have a dream about him, God is speaking to me about a mentality of provision. See, the dream is not about him. He is a symbol. Another example would be if you have a dream about someone who you know struggles with manipulation. God may not be warning you about that specific person. If that person symbolizes manipulation to you, then God could be warning you by communicating that the enemy has a scheme to bring people around you who have manipulative motives.

As we have dreams about specific people, our job is to ask Holy Spirit if this dream is literally about that person. If it is not, then we need to ask Him what that person is a symbol of, and what God is trying to communicate.

Emotions

Often when I am interpreting dreams, one of the first questions I will frequently ask is, "Are there any emotions that stuck out to you in your dream?" Understanding our emotions in dreams is a powerful key in discerning whether or not a dream is from the Lord. Emotions can also show us what God's purpose is behind the dream.

There are two types of emotions that we can have while dreaming. There are emotions forced on us by the enemy, and there are emotions that are provoked by the Lord. The difference is that one type of emotion is external, whereas the other is internal. When emotions such as fear, anxiety, and insecurity are being externally placed upon us in dreams, this is a clear sign that a dream is not from the Lord. This is the enemy trying to place us in emotional bondage in our dreams. This is very different than the Lord internally provoking emotions that are already occurring in our heart.

God can also give us dreams where we are experiencing emotions such as fear, anxiety, insecurity, etc. The difference is that in these dreams, God is placing His finger on emotions that are already stirring in our heart for the purpose of bringing freedom and healing. This is why I will often ask people if any emotions stuck out to them in their dreams. It tells me if the Lord wanted to use this dream to minister inner healing.

Symbols

A

Abdominal Area: Core values. Discernment.

Abortion: The enemy trying to put God's plan to death.

Academics: Training from the Lord. Testing from the Lord.

Accident: The enemy trying to derail something from the Lord. Fear. Anxiety.

Acid: The Lord wanting to dissolve a plan in motion. The enemy trying to snuff out something that the Lord has planned.

Acoustic Guitar: A call to worship. A seasoned anointing. Musical anointing. Creativity. A call to the arts. A time of self-expression.

Actor: Dishonesty. Two-faced. Creativity. A call to the arts.

Addiction: Bondage. Something that the Lord wants to bring freedom from.

Administration: God bringing order. Divine systems.

Adolescence: Lack of maturity. Newness.

Unlocking the Language of Dreams

Adoption: God bringing a revelation of sonship or daughtership.

Adult: Maturity.

Adultery: Sin. Rebellion. An attack on marriage.

Advisor: God bringing direction and clarity. A message of wisdom from the Lord.

Aerial View: Obtaining God's perspective on a situation.

Airplane: A call to the nations. Transition. Travelling. A large ministry.

Airport: God preparing an individual for a commissioning. A call to the nations. Transition. Travelling.

Alarm: Warning. Urgency. The timing of the Lord.

Album: A literal album being created and recorded. Professionalism. Influence.

Alley: Hidden activity. Work behind the scenes.

Alligator: Spiritual attack. Gossip. Lies.

Aloe Vera: The Lord bringing healing.

Amber: The glory of God. Refinement.

Ancestors: History. Legacy. Inheritance. Generational blessings. Generational curses.

Dream Interpretation Dictionary

Anchor: Hope (Hebrews 6:19). Stability. A season of stillness.

Angel: Messenger from God. Protection. Ministering spirit.

Animals: A variety of species of animals together can symbolize different giftings and anointings working together.

Ankle: An area of weakness in an individual's life.

Anointing Oil: God anointing for a specific task or mandate. Healing.

Ant: A time of busyness. Work.

Antibiotics: The Lord bringing healing.

Antidote: God giving the solution for a problem.

Apartment: A temporary season or circumstance.

Appetizer: Revelation. God preparing for something new.

Apple: Spiritual nourishment. Temptation.

Aquarium: The call over an individual's life. God increasing an evangelistic anointing.

Argument: Conflict in relationships. Spiritual warfare. False accusations.

Ark: A season of building with the Lord. God declaring a new work.

Arm: The work of the Lord through an individual. The reach of an individual's influence.

Armour: The Lord's protection. Preparation for an endeavor. An individual being equipped for their calling.

Army: God's army. Strategy from God.

Arrow: God's justice (Psalm 64:7). The enemy's accusations (Ephesians 6:16). Spiritual children (Psalm 127:4).

Art: Creativity. Co-creating with God.

Attic: Memories. History.

Autograph: Solidifying and establishing a work.

Autumn: Transition.

Axe: Tool of warfare.

B

Baby: A new ministry.

Badge: Authority. Honour.

Baggage: Bondage. Something the Lord wants to bring freedom to.

Dream Interpretation Dictionary

Bagpipe: Something coming to an end. Mourning.

Bakery: Fresh revelation.

Bald: God wanting to bring clarity concerning identity. Maturity.

Balloon: Celebration. Childlikeness. Joy.

Ballroom: Romancing with the Lord. Intimacy. Generational blessing.

Banana: Fruit of the Spirit (Galatians 5:22-23).

Bank: God's storehouse of blessing.

Banner: Something God has declared over an individual's life.

Barefoot: Holiness (Exodus 3:5). Authenticity. God wanting to bring clarity concerning calling and destiny. A poverty mentality.

Barbecue: Community. Connection in relationships. Mature revelation.

Barrenness: God wanting to bring fruitfulness in an area of life.

Base: God doing a foundational work.

Basement: The depths of the heart. The soul (mind, will and emotions).

Bat: Schemes of the enemy. Witchcraft.

Unlocking the Language of Dreams

Bath: A time of cleansing. A season of reflection.

Bathroom: A time of cleansing.

Baton: A time of commissioning into calling. Generations working together. Running the race with perseverance (Hebrews 12:1).

Battery (Full): God giving energy. Grace and stamina for a specific task.

Battery (Empty): A sign of over exerting energy. Fatigue.

Beach: A time of rest. A time of reflection.

Bear: God silencing a mocking spirit (2 Kings 2:22-24). Religious spirit. Principality.

Beard: Maturity. Unity (Psalm 133:2).

Beaver: A season of busyness. A time to build for the Lord.

Bed: Intimacy. Rest. God could use a bed to speak to an individual's dream life.

Bedroom: Your intimate walk with the Lord. Marriage.

Bee: A season of busyness and work. A season to receive new revelation, as honey is often symbolic of revelation.

Bell: The sound of the Lord, God's prophetic decree.

Dream Interpretation Dictionary

Belt: Truth (Ephesians 6:14). Something that holds everything together.

Bib: A time to grow in foundational truths.

Bible: God's word. A time to renewing the mind in what the word of God says.

Bicycle: Revelation.

Bird (Flying): Freedom. Going to new heights in the Lord. Seeing circumstances from a bird's eye view.

Bird (Caged): Bondage. An insecurity concerning an individual's calling and destiny.

Birthing: God birthing something either in an individual's life, or through them.

Black (Positive side): Mysteries of God.

Black (Negative side): Bondage. Spiritual warfare. Deception. Demonic stronghold.

Black Cat: Witchcraft.

Blade: Skill. Discernment. Gossip. Word curses.

Blemish: God wanting to refine or cleanse an area of life.

Blindness: Lack of clarity in a situation or circumstance. Pride.

Unlocking the Language of Dreams

Blizzard: A winter season of life. Lack of clarity in circumstances. A chaotic circumstance. Warning. Purity.

Blood: The blood of Jesus. Forgiveness. Cleansing. Protection.

Blue (Positive side): Revelation. Wisdom. Holy Spirit. The prophetic ministry.

Blue (Negative side): Depression. Sadness. Confusion.

Blueprint: God's divine strategy.

Boat: A call to venture into the unknown. Adventure. Ministry.

Bomb: The power of God. Scheme of the enemy.

Bones: Vision that God wants to give life to. An area of life that God wants to mature.

Book: Knowledge. Wisdom. Revelation.

Bookshelf: Advanced revelation. An ordained time of learning something new.

Boots: Being equipped to walk out one's calling. Protection from the enemy's schemes.

Boss: A figure of authority.

Boulder: An obstacle.

Dream Interpretation Dictionary

Bowl: The portion or capacity that God has given an individual.

Box: Unhealthy expectations from others. Unhealthy limits or restrictions.

Branch: Abiding in God. Learning a lifestyle of resting.

Brass: Something that the Lord has brought refinement to.

Bread: Spiritual food. The word of God.

Breath: God bringing life.

Breeze: Winds of change. Transition. A time of refreshing.

Brick: A gift, anointing, skill or ability. Small hindrances of the enemy.

Brick Wall: Different gifts, anointings, skills, or abilities working together. Something preventing a person from walking in their full inheritance in the Lord.

Bride: The bride of Christ. The church. New understanding of identity.

Bridegroom: Jesus.

Bridge: Partnership. Reconciliation in relationships.

Briefcase: Anointing for business. God bringing order to work or ministry.

Unlocking the Language of Dreams

Broom: A time to focus on cleaning up a mess, whether that is in a ministry, business, circumstances, relationships, etc.

Brown: Maturity. Humility. Meekness.

Brush: Something that God is using to refine an individual's perception of their identity.

Buffet: Our access to the kingdom of heaven through the cross. Fresh revelation.

Building: The kingdom of heaven. The church. An individual's ministry or business.

Bullet: Gossip. Lies. Accusation from the enemy. Weapon of warfare.

Burden: Something that the Lord wants to bring freedom to.

Burr: A person or circumstance that is causing hindrances.

Bus: Transition. A local ministry.

Butterfly: Transformation. Maturity. Healing.

C

Cabin: Intimacy with God. A time of rest. A poverty mentality. Seclusion.

Cage: An area of life where an individual does not feel free. An area of life where an individual does not feel as though they can express themselves.

Cake: God celebrating a milestone of an individual's life. Tasting the goodness of God.

Calendar: The Lord's timing. God's plans for an individual's month, season, year or life.

Camel: Provision. Wealth. Longevity.

Camera: God wanting an individual to take note of something specific. Memories. Reflection. God wanting an individual to focus their attention.

Cancer: Literal sickness. Spiritual sickness. Spiritual warfare. Unhealthiness in an area of life.

Candle: God bringing clarity in a trying season. Influence with others. God revealing truth.

Canon: The spiritual battle taking place.

Cape: Mantle. Calling.

Car: Ministry.

Cards: Community. Relational connection. Strategy.

Unlocking the Language of Dreams

Cash: The Lord's provision. Influence. Inheritance.

Casino: Unhealthy risks. Compromise.

Casket: The Lord putting a carnal mentality to death. Something coming to an end. The enemy trying to stop the work of the Lord.

Castle: An individual having understanding concerning their royal identity. Influence. God's kingdom. Man-made kingdom.

Cat: Independent spirit. Witchcraft.

Catapult: God launching an individual into new things.

Caterpillar: Training season. Lack of maturity.

Cave: Hiddenness. Humility. Friendship with the Lord.

Cavern: The realm of the soul.

Ceiling: A feeling of an inability to go higher. Unhealthy expectations from others.

Cell Phone: Communication. Prayer.

Cello: Musical anointing. Creativity. A time of self-expression.

Cement: Something solidified by the Lord. Stubbornness.

Chain: Unity. Bondage.

Dream Interpretation Dictionary

Chainsaw: The Lord tearing down an old way of doing things. The enemy trying to enforce fear.

Cheetah: A time of acceleration.

Cheque: Financial provision. God resourcing vision.

Chess: The Lord's strategy. Wisdom from God.

Child: A maturing ministry. Faith. Childlikeness. Childishness.

Childbearing: Carrying or birthing something significant for God's kingdom.

Church Building: A literal church. The body of Christ. The kingdom of God. Religious spirit.

Cigarette: An unhealthy habit that the Lord wants to change.

Circle: Covenant. Feeling stuck in a certain pattern of life.

City: A literal city. The kingdom of God. The kingdom of darkness.

Clinic: Healing. Restoration. God bringing health to a specific area of life.

Cloak: Mantle. Calling.

Clock: The timing of the Lord.

Closet: Something hidden that the Lord wants to bring to light.

Unlocking the Language of Dreams

Clothes (Old): A poverty mentality. Having a false perception of self. Shame.

Clothes (New): Promotion. Seeing yourself the way God sees you. Newfound confidence. Influence.

Cloud: The mysteries of God. The glory of God. Holiness.

Clown: Fear. Anxiety. Deception. Joy.

Construction: The Lord building something. Reformation.

Coal: Preparation for what the Lord is about to do. Preparation for the igniting of a move of the Spirit.

Coat: Calling. Destiny. The Father's blessing.

Coffee: Energy. Perseverance. Unhealthy dependency.

Coffin: Something coming to an end. Leaving a past season behind.

Comb: Something that God is using to refine an individual's perception of their identity.

Comet: God bringing warning of either the enemy's schemes or upcoming circumstances.

Compass: God bringing clarity concerning direction.

Computer: Influence. An anointing for technology.

Cot: Poverty mentality.

Dream Interpretation Dictionary

Couch: Rest. Counsel from the Lord. A time of inner healing. Self-care.

Cracked Foundation: Flaw in an individual's perception of themselves. Flaw in an individual's perception of God. Flaw in character. Heart wound.

Cradle: God nurturing the calling over an individual's life. The need to take care of a new ministry.

Cross: Jesus. Sacrifice. Dying to self.

Crow: Demonic opposition.

Crown: Royal identity. Authority.

Cup: The portion or capacity that God has given an individual.

D

Dam: Something preventing a move of the Spirit. Something preventing an outpour of blessing.

Dance: Creativity. Worship. Victory. Intercession.

Dart: The accusations of the enemy. Lies. Gossip. Manipulative thoughts or prayers.

Day Planner: A focus on time management.

Unlocking the Language of Dreams

Deafness: A lack of ability to hear God. A lack of willingness to hear truth. Stubbornness. Pride.

Death: Something coming to an end. Leaving a past season behind.

Deer: Peace. Provision. Desire and hunger for the Lord (Psalm 42:1).

Dentist: God bringing alignment. Stronghold of fear.

Dentures: False knowledge, wisdom or revelation.

Desert: Bondage. Testing from the Lord.

Dessert: Enjoying the goodness of God.

Desk: Work. An individual's career. An anointing for writing. Godly order.

Dew: Intimacy with the Lord (Genesis 2:6). A new beginning.

Diamond: Purity. Refinement. Faithfulness.

Diary: Process. Journey. Vulnerability.

Dice: Healthy risk taking. Unhealthy risk taking.

Diet: A mentality of looking for a quick fix.

Dinner: New revelation. A revelation of the family of God. The realm of relationships.

Dream Interpretation Dictionary

Dirt: An area of life that has not been cleansed. Something buried and hidden that needs to come to light.

Disguise: Dishonesty. Two-faced. Deception.

Dishwasher: A time of cleansing. Inner healing.

Diving: Seeking the depths and mysteries of God. A call to step into the unknown.

Divorce: Division in marriage. Spiritual attack on marriage or relationship. Broken covenant. Divisive spirit.

Dock: Overcoming fear. Peace.

Dog: Loyalty. Friendship. The realm of relationships.

Doll: Symbol of childhood. Innocence. Childlikeness.

Door: Opportunity.

Doorbell: A call to pursue opportunities. A new relationship.

Downstairs: The soul. Depths of the Lord. Taking a step back.

Dolphin: Commitment. Loyalty. Assistance. Protection.

Dragon: Pride. Majesty.

Drapes: Hiddenness in the Lord. Boundaries in relationships. Hidden sin.

Unlocking the Language of Dreams

Dress: Understanding daughtership. Identity. Self-worth.

Drums: Breakthrough anointing. Worship. Musical anointing. Creativity. A time of self-expression.

Dryer: The Lord completing a time of cleansing and healing.

Dumbbell: Growth and training concerning calling, gifting, anointing, skills or abilities.

Dungeon: Bondage.

Dynamite: The power of God.

E

Eagle: The prophetic ministry. The ability to rise above circumstances. Heavenly perspective.

Ear: Ability to hear the Lord.

Earmuff: Lack of ability to hear the Lord.

Earth: God's global plan. Worldly way of thinking.

Earthquake: God shaking things that need to be shaken.

Dream Interpretation Dictionary

Echo: The Lord reiterating something He is already speaking.

Edge: A call to take a risk. Living too close to the edge. Compromise. Caution. Recklessness.

Education: Training for calling. A time of testing from the Lord. A fear of failure.

Eel: Trickery of the enemy.

Egg (In Shell): Vision that is in the preparation and planning stage.

Egg (Out of Shell): Vision that is coming into fruition.

Election: A literal election taking place. God promoting an individual into greater influence.

Electric Guitar: A new anointing. Worship. Musical anointing. Creativity. A time of self-expression.

Electricity: The power of God (Habakkuk 3:4).

Elderly: Wisdom. Experience. Generational blessing. Generational curse.

Eldest: The blessing of a firstborn.

Engine: The heart of a ministry, business, etc.

Entrance: The beginning of a new season. Invitation into something new. Opportunity.

Envelope: A message from the Lord.

Equipment: A time of training and equipping.

Eraser: Forgiveness. A change in direction.

Exit: The end of a season.

Extinguisher: A time to focus on cleaning up a mess, whether that is in a ministry, business, circumstances, relationships, etc. The Lord putting out fires.

Eyes: Seeing what the Lord sees. A seer anointing. A prophetic anointing. Increased discernment.

Eyehole: God giving clarity in a specific situation. People's eyes being on a circumstance that should not be.

F

Faceless Person: The Father. Jesus. Holy Spirit. Angel. Demon.

Falling: God could be exposing fear and anxiety in the dreamer's life. God may be exposing the dreamer's feelings of not being in control of their life.

Famine: Lack of spiritual food. Fear of lack. Poverty mentality.

Dream Interpretation Dictionary

Farmer/ Farming: God tilling the soil of an individual's heart to ready them for what the Lord wants to do.

Father: The Father heart of God. Literal father. Father figure.

Fatigue: Lack of energy. God wanting rest to be a priority.

Fashion: Creativity. Favour with man. Promotion.

Feather: Favour. Angels. The Lord's protection (Psalm 91:4). Anointing for writing.

Feline: Independent spirit. witchcraft.

Fig: Temptation. Fruit of the Spirit.

Fire: Holy Spirit. Baptism of the Spirit. Revival. Refiner's fire. Chastening. Discipline of the Lord.

Fireworks: The celebration of a milestone in life. Victory.

Firstborn: The blessing of a firstborn. First fruit of revival.

Fish: Evangelism. Schemes of the enemy.

Flag: Worship. Victory.

Flint: A renewed mind (Ezekiel 3:9).

Flood: The love of God. A move of the Spirit. A sense of being overwhelmed. A fear of not being in control.

Unlocking the Language of Dreams

Floor: Platform. Foundational work. Humility.

Flower: The fragrance of God. Gift from God.

Flute: Musical anointing. Heavenly sounds. Worship.

Flying: Rising above circumstances. Going to new heights with the Lord. Heaven's perspective.

Fog: Confusion. Lack of clarity. Mysteries of God.

Foot: Advancement of the gospel. Moving forward in calling.

Forest: Wilderness season. Intimacy with the Lord. Adventure with God. Depression.

Fork: A fork in the road in life. A time of decision-making.

Fossil: History. Long forgotten truths and revelation.

Fox: The enemy trying to prevent multiplication of fruit (Song of Songs 2:15). Subtle attacks from the enemy.

Foundation: Identity in Christ. The beginning stages of building a ministry, business, etc.

Fountain: A time of refreshing with the Lord.

Foyer: The realm of relationships. Connections. New relationships.

Freezer: The Lord preserving something for a later time.

Frog: Demonic hindrances.

Fruit: The fruit of one's life or ministry. Fruits of the Spirit (Galatians 5:22-23).

Fuel: Holy Spirit. The things that fuel an individual's life. The input or influence from others in an individual's life.

Fugitive: An individual running from wounds of the heart.

Funeral: Something coming to an end. Leaving a past season behind.

Furnace: The refining of the Lord. Discipline from the Lord.

Furniture (Old): An older way of doing things. Generational blessings. Generational curses.

Furniture (New): A newer way of doing things. Generational blessings. Generational curses.

G

Garbage: Something that God wants to get rid of in an individual's life.

Garden: The heart. The core of an individual. Heaven. Intimacy and friendship with God.

Unlocking the Language of Dreams

Game: Friendship with God. Rest. Joy. The enemy trying to manipulate someone.

Gang: Demonic opposition.

Gas: Holy Spirit. The things that fuel an individual's life. The input or influence from others in an individual's life.

Gas Station: Holy Spirit. The input of others. The things that fuel an individual's life.

Gate (Closed): The Lord's protection. Something being preserved for a later time.

Gate (Open): An open door. Opportunity.

Gemstone: Gifting. Anointing. Calling. The promises of God. The blessings of God.

Generations: Generational blessing. Legacy. Generational curse.

Ghost: The demonic trying to trick, bring confusion or manipulate.

Giant: A seemingly large obstacle. A test or circumstance that God wants to use to train and equip. Demonic opposition.

Gift: A gift from God. Impartation from the one giving the gift.

Ginger: Healing. Cleansing.

Glass: Transparency. Vulnerability.

Glasses: The Lord causing an individual to see life through a new lens.

Globe: God's strategy for the earth.

Glove: A position that fits who an individual is perfectly.

Glue: Unity. Partnership. Covenant.

Gold: Refinement. Godly character. Finances. Wealth.

Golden Retriever: Friend. Loyalty. The realm of relationships.

Goose: Working as a team. Canada.

Government: Literal government. Spiritual government. God's appointed leaders.

Gown: Understanding daughtership. Identity. Self-worth.

Graduation: Promotion. Affirmation from God the Father.

Grandfather Clock: Inheritance. God's divine timing. Generational blessing. Generational curse.

Grape: Fruit of the Spirit (Galatians 5:22-23).

Grass: Peace. Rest.

Graveyard: Dreams that have died. Generational blessings. Generational curses.

Green: Growth. New life. Creativity. Promise. The pastoral ministry.

Greenhouse: Rapid growth.

Grocery Store: A time of advanced revelation.

Guard: Angel. Protection.

Guest in Home (Wanted): Partnership. Key relationship. Unity.

Guest in Home (Unwanted): Boundaries. God could be bringing warning concerning this person.

Guide: Holy Spirit. Angel. Divine direction. Clarity concerning direction.

Guitar: Musical anointing. Creativity. Worship. A time of self-expression.

Gun: Power. Authority.

Gym: A time of training with the Lord.

H

Hair: Identity.

Hairbrush: Something that God is using to refine an individual's perception of their identity.

Dream Interpretation Dictionary

Hallway: Transition.

Hammer: The word of the Lord (Jeremiah 23:29).

Hand (Right): Power. Authority (Mark 16:19). Inheritance (Genesis 48:14). The Father's blessing. Promotion.

Hand (Left): A time of training and equipping.

Hammock: An ordained time of rest.

Handcuffs: Bondage.

Hardhat: Renewing the mind. A time of building with the Lord.

Harp: Holiness. Heavenly sounds.

Harvest: Salvation. A time of increased evangelism.

Hat: Spiritual accountability. Revelation.

Haunted House: Heart wounds. Generational curses. Demonic opposition.

Hawk: Greater vision to see what the Lord is doing. The Lord's protection.

Head: Jesus (Colossians 1:18). Authority figure. An anointing to teach. God highlighting a specific mentality. Knowledge.

Headphones: The Lord declaring a new sound. A time of introspectiveness and reflection. Avoidance of truth being spoken.

Unlocking the Language of Dreams

Heart: Desires of the heart. Passions of the heart. Heart wound.

Hedge: The Lord's protection (Job 1:10).

Helicopter: Demonic power.

Helmet: Renewing the mind.

Herald: Angel. Messenger.

Herb: Healing. Spiritual health. Emotional health. Physical health.

Hill: A test from the Lord. A specific circumstance. A trying circumstance.

Hole: A trap from the enemy.

Honey: Revelation. Clarity to see (1 Samuel 14:27). God's promises over an individual's life.

Hook: A trap from the enemy. Manipulation.

Horn: Authority (Revelation 5:6).

Horse: Move of the Holy Spirit. Power. Authority.

Hotel: A temporary season or circumstance.

House: A symbol of the dreamer's life.

Husband: Jesus. Literal husband. Spiritual covering.

Dream Interpretation Dictionary

I

Ice: A time to be cautious.

Idol: Something held above God.

Illegal Activity: False accusation from the enemy. Holy Spirit bringing conviction concerning compromise.

Illusion: Deception of the enemy. Things not being as they seem.

Illustration: Teaching from the Lord. Artistic ability.

Incubator: A time of preparation.

Industrial: A time of reconstruction in a ministry, business or person.

Ink: The Lord bringing definition. Being marked by God. Accusations or labels of the enemy. Worldly labels.

Interior: The soul (mind, will and emotions). The heart.

Insect: Things that an individual may be giving too much attention to. Annoyances.

Iron: Something made of lasting quality. Longevity.

Island: Independent spirit. Literal island.

J

Jacket: Calling. Destiny. The Father's blessing. Mantle.

Jar: The Lord preserving something of importance in an individual's life.

Jail: Bondage. Feeling trapped. Worldly mentality. Addiction.

Jet: A time of acceleration.

Jewel (Depending on the colour of the jewel): Royalty. God's glory. Provision.

Jewelry: Desires of the heart. Precious things to the heart. Wealth.

Jigsaw Puzzle: An individual discovering how they fit within the kingdom of God. God bringing direction concerning confusing circumstances.

Journal: Process. Journey. Vulnerability.

Juice: Time of refreshing. God developing the fruits of the Spirit.

K

Kale: Health. A time of cleansing.

Kangaroo: Nurturing. A pastoral heart. The maternal heart of God. Australia.

Keepsake: Something precious to the heart.

Kettle: Preparation.

Keyboard: An anointing to write.

Keyhole: Something that the Lord wants to reveal and unlock.

Keys: Authority (Matthew 16:19). Wisdom.

Kitchen: Preparation. Health. Spiritual nourishment.

Kite: A time of dreaming with God. Receiving new vision.

Knife: Gossip. Word curses. Skill. Discernment.

Knight: A call to the service of God.

Knighted: God's affirmation. Promotion.

Knot: Confusion. God establishing something.

Knuckles: Conflict. Aggression. Warfare.

L

Label: Identity. God wanting to bring definition to something.

Laboratory: New ideas. Creativity. A time of trying out new things. A time to explore new options.

Labyrinth: Confusion. A sense of running around in circles.

Lamb: Jesus, the Lamb of God (John 1:29). Compassion. Empathy. A pastoral heart for people.

Ladder: Jesus (Genesis 28:12). Promotion. New revelation.

Lake: Peace. Resting in the Lord. Intimacy with the Lord.

Lamp: Clarity. Evangelism. Preaching the Gospel.

Laptop: An anointing for technology. An anointing to write. Influence.

Laundry (Dirty): A sense of shame. Embarrassment. Having a false perception of self.

Laundry (Clean): Promotion. An individual seeing themselves the way God sees them. Newfound confidence.

Lava: Caution. Warning.

Lead: Weighty truth. Authority.

Leather: Something made of good quality. Something manmade. Striving.

Lemon: Cleansing.

Leaf: Healing to the nations (Revelation 22:2).

Leaves Falling: Transition. Change in season.

Ledge: A call to take a risk. Living too close to the edge. Compromise. Caution.

Library: A season of learning and training. History.

Lifeboat: Support. Freedom. Redemption.

Lifeline: Support. Freedom. Redemption.

Light: The glory of God. Revelation. Insight.

Lightening - The power of God.

Lighthouse: Guidance. Being a light in a dark place.

Lion: The Lion of Judah. Victory. Power. Authority. The apostolic ministry.

Living Room: The realm of relationships.

Lizard: Deception. Lies.

Lock: The mysteries of God. An area where breakthrough is needed. The feeling of an inability to move forward.

Luggage: Transition. A call to the nations. A call to rest. Bondage (baggage). Something the Lord wants to bring freedom to.

M

Machine (Old): An old way of doing things.

Machine (New): A new way of doing things.

Magazine: Gossip. Lies. Informative information.

Magnet: Something that an individual is attracted to, either with positive or negative influence.

Mail: A message from the Lord.

Mango: Fruit of the Spirit (Galatians 5:22-23).

Manhole: A season of hiddenness. The Lord's protection.

Mantle: Calling. Mandate. Destiny.

Market: Influence in the marketplace. Opportunities.

Marriage: Partnership. Covenant relationship.

Mask: False perception of identity. Lies. Two-faced.

Mast: God bringing direction. Realignment.

Dream Interpretation Dictionary

Match: God about to ignite something.

Mattress: Rest. Intimacy with God.

Maze: Confusion. A sense of running around in circles.

Medal: Authority. Honour. Recognition. Affirmation.

Medication: Healing. Restoration.

Memorial: Honour. Respect. History. Legacy.

Metal: Something made of lasting quality. Longevity.

Meteoroid: God bringing warning of either the enemy's schemes or upcoming circumstances.

Metronome: The timing of the Lord. Keeping in step with the Spirit.

Microphone: Communication. The message of the Lord.

Microscope: A call to look at situations more closely.

Microwave: The preparation of the Lord. A time of acceleration.

Milk: God's promises over an individual's life. Foundational teachings (1 Corinthians 3:2).

Mine: The deep things of the heart of God. A time of hiddenness. A time of busyness.

Mirror: An individual's perspective of themselves. A call to examine the heart.

Mold: Caution. Something subtle that is unhealthy.

Moon: The church. Jesus. Principality.

Mother: The maternal heart of God. Literal mother. Nurturing. Mother figure.

Motorcycle: Revelation that will take you from one place to another. Things moving at an accelerated pace. Adventure.

Mouse: Subtle schemes of the enemy. A time of hiddenness.

Mouth: A call to speak the word of the Lord. The prophetic ministry. Worship anointing. Gossip. Lies. Jezebel spirit.

Mountain: Intimacy with the Lord. Influence. A specific realm of society. The call over an individual's life. Obstacle.

N

Nail: Something being finalized. Something coming to a close.

Neck: Support for those in leadership.

Necklace: Desires of the heart. Precious things to the heart. Wealth.

Dream Interpretation Dictionary

Needle: Fear. Anxiety. Healing.

Nest: The nurturing heart of God. God nurturing an individual's calling. A time to receive and to be cared for.

Newspaper: Important information. Something taking place that should be taken note of.

Nightclub: A literal nightclub. Rebellion. The kingdom of darkness.

Nightgown - Rest. God could use a nightgown to speak to an individual's dream life.

Nose: Discernment.

Notebook: A time to learn new things. A season of training.

Novel: The story of the dreamer's life. An anointing to write.

Nudity: Vulnerability. Intimacy with God. Shame. Vulnerability to the enemy's tactics.

O

Oar: Revelation. Something given by God to help an individual persevere.

Obstacle: An obstacle in life. A mindset that an

individual must learn to overcome.

Ocean: The depths of God. The majesty of God. Adventure. A call to the unknown.

Octopus: A unique way of God working. The enemy trying to entangle or entrap.

Office: Career. Work. The realm of finances. A five-fold ministry office (Ephesians 4:11-12).

Offspring: Literal children. Spiritual children. The fruit of an individual's life. Ministry.

Oil: Holy Spirit. The things that fuel an individual's life. Input or influence from others.

Orange - Colour (Positive side): Vision. Celebration. Harvest. Evangelism.

Orange - Colour (Negative side): Lack of maturity. Witchcraft.

Orange (Fruit): Fruit of the spirit (Galatians 5:22-23).

Orchestra: Teamwork. Creativity. The sound of the Lord.

Oven: The preparation of the Lord.

Owl: The prophetic ministry. Seeing prophetically in the marketplace. Wisdom.

Ox: Godly character. A servant heart.

P

Package: A gift from God. Impartation from the one giving the gift.

Padlock: The mysteries of God's heart. An area where breakthrough is needed. The feeling of an inability to move forward.

Painting: Creativity. Co-creating with God. An anointing for the arts.

Pajama: Symbol of childhood. Innocence. Childlikeness. Season of rest.

Paper (Blank): The beginning of something new.

Paper (Not Blank): An established work.

Paperclip: The Lord holding something together.

Park: Symbol of an individual's childhood. Joy. Innocence.

Path: Symbol of an individual's life. A specific season. Journey.

Peak: New heights with God. Friendship with God. Influence. Promotion.

Pear: Fruit of the Spirit (Galatians 5:22-23).

Pedestal: Idol. Unhealthy expectations.

Pen: An established work. Anointing to write.

Unlocking the Language of Dreams

Pencil: A work that is not definitive. Artistic ability. Anointing to write.

Perfume: The fragrance of the Lord. Intercession. Prayer. Worship.

Pew: A time of learning new things. Receiving instruction. Complacency.

Pharmacy: Healing. Restoration. Caution.

Phone: Communication. Prayer.

Photo: A time to take note of something important. A time of reflection.

Piano: Musical anointing. Creativity. Worship. A time of self-expression.

Pig: God highlighting something that is out of order. Arrogance.

Pillar: Godly character. Godly people. Divine relationship.

Pistol: Power. Authority. Spiritual attack.

Pizza: Community. Connection in relationships.

Plane: Travelling. A call to the nations. A call to missions.

Plowing: Forerunner calling. Pioneer anointing. A sense of going where no one has yet gone. Perseverance.

Dream Interpretation Dictionary

Pocket: Something hidden that the Lord either wants to remain hidden, or bring to light.

Polar Bear: Aggressive spiritual warfare. Principality.

Police officer: Angels. Authority. Authority figure.

Predator: Fear. Anxiety.

Pregnancy: Carrying something significant for God's kingdom. Carrying people's expectations.

Present: A gift from God. Impartation from the one giving the gift.

Prison: Bondage. Feeling trapped. Worldly mentality. Addiction.

Prize: A gift from the Lord. The Lord's provision.

Pulpit: An anointing to communicate. Church leadership. Church government. Ordained platform for an individual.

Puppet: Manipulation. Control.

Purple: Royalty. Identity.

Purse: The realm of finances. Wealth.

Puzzle: An individual discovering how they fit within the kingdom of God. God bringing direction concerning confusing circumstances. God putting the pieces of an individual's life together.

Pyramid: Demonic stronghold. Bondage. Obstacle.

Q

Quail: Provision from the Lord.

Queen: A revelation of daughtership. A revelation of royalty. Principality.

Quicksand: A trap set by the enemy. The sense of not being in control in life.

Quiver: God's justice (Psalm 64:7). The enemy's accusations (Ephesians 6:16). Spiritual children (Psalm 127:4).

R

Rabbit: Acceleration. Innocence.

Racetrack: Perseverance. Calling. Destiny.

Radio: An increase of influence.

Raft: A ministry in its infancy stage.

Railroad: The foundation work of a move of the Spirit of God.

Raisin: Seasoned fruit of the Spirit (Galatians 5:22-23).

Dream Interpretation Dictionary

Rain: Holy Spirit. A time of cleansing. A time of refreshing. A time of growth.

Rainbow: God's promises. God's covenant (Genesis 9:13).

Rat: Contagious dysfunction. Schemes of the enemy.

Raven: Demonic opposition.

Recorder: God wanting an individual to take note of something He is communicating.

Red (Positive side): Power. Authority. The blood of Jesus. Mercy. The apostolic ministry.

Red (Negative side): Anxiety. Pride. Aggression.

Refrigerator: Something that the Lord is preserving for a later time.

Rib: Spouse. Something that God is using to protect an individual's heart.

Ribbon (Depending on Colour). Anointing. Revelation.

Ribcage: Something that God is using to protect an individual's heart.

Ring: Covenant.

River: The kingdom of heaven. The ways of God. Mercy. Grace.

Road: A symbol of an individual's life. A specific season.

Robe: Mantle. Revelation of royalty.

Rock: Jesus. Stability.

Roof: Spiritual accountability. Other people's unhealthy expectations. Limitations that someone may feel.

Rope: Strength. Support. Unity.

Rowboat: A ministry in its infancy stage.

Ruler: Preparation for increase. Testing from the Lord. Comparison. A mentality of someone measuring themselves to others. Fear. Anxiety.

Running: Acceleration. Perseverance. Avoidance from issues of the heart.

S

Sackcloth: Repentance. Prayer. Intercession.

Safe House: The Lord's protection. God declaring a time of hiddenness and inner healing.

Sail: God bringing direction. Realignment.

Dream Interpretation Dictionary

Sailboat: God bringing direction. Realignment. Adventure.

Salad: Physical health. Emotional health. Spiritual health.

Salt: An individual's ability to influence those around them. An attempt to preserve a past season.

Salve: Healing. Protection.

Sash: Affirmation from the Lord. Favour with God. Favour with man.

Saw: Chastening of the Lord (John 15:2). Refining from the Lord.

Scabbard: An anointing that is not currently being utilized.

Scales: Deception. An inability to see clearly (Acts 9:18).

Scarecrow: Fear. Anxiety. Something or someone the Lord is using to protect His work.

Scent: Discernment.

Sceptre: God's authority over the nations (Revelation 2:26). Our call to reign with God (Revelation 2:26-27). Authority. A revelation of royal identity.

Scarf: The Lord's protection.

School: Testing from the Lord. A season of training. A fear of failure.

Unlocking the Language of Dreams

Scribe: A call to take note of what the Lord is saying.

Scroll: The strategy of God. A prophetic mandate.

Sea: The depths of God. The majesty of God. Adventure. A call to the unknown.

Seal: The Lord establishing a work.

Seed: New revelation. A call to be faithful with the little.

Shampoo: A time of cleansing.

Sheep: Healing in the realm of the soul. Obedience. Those who someone may be called to pastor.

Shepherd: Jesus. The pastoral ministry.

Shield: The Lord's protection. Faith (Ephesians 6:16).

Ship: Ministry.

Shipwreck: Ministries that have fallen or failed.

Shoe: Something that an individual is called to walk in. Anointing. The ability to advance the kingdom of God.

Shoulder: Government (Isaiah 9:6). Burden bearing. Legacy.

Shovel: A call to uncover new truth. A call to uncover lies.

Shower: The Lord bringing cleansing.

Dream Interpretation Dictionary

Sidewalk: Something on the sidelines.

Signet Ring: Authority (Haggai 2:23). The Father's blessing (Luke 15:22). Inheritance.

Silver: Redemption. Restoration. Finances.

Skeleton: Vision that God wants to give life to. An area of life that God wants to mature.

Skunk: Schemes of the enemy. The enemy attempting to taint the work of the Lord.

Sky: Rising above circumstances. Going to new heights with the Lord.

Skyscraper: A specific ministry or church. The call to see life from a different perspective.

Slingshot: The Lord readying for acceleration and commissioning.

Snake: The enemy. Warfare. Deception. Lies.

Snow: Purity. Holiness. Cleansing. A time where God is growing character.

Soap: A time of cleansing.

Soil: The condition of someone's heart. The spiritual atmosphere where an individual is called to build for God.

Speaker: An increase of influence.

Spear: Power. Authority. Weapon of warfare.

Spider: Lies. A trap from the enemy.

Spiderweb: Lies. A trap from the enemy.

Spine: The foundation or backbone of an individual's life, ministry, career, etc.

Staircase: God bringing an individual to higher places.

Stars: Angels (Revelations 1:20). The fruit of an individual's life (Genesis 26:4). Legacy.

Statue: Honour. Respect. History. Legacy.

Stereo: An increase of influence.

Stone: Hard heartedness. A refined mindset.

Stream: An aspect of God's nature. Peace.

Street: Symbol of an individual's life. A specific season.

Subway: A move of God. Plans that are not yet revealed. The underground church.

Suit: Business anointing. Influence. Promotion.

Sun: Jesus. The Father. Power. The Refiner's fire.

Sunblock: Caution.

Sunglasses: The Lord causing an individual to see life through a new lens.

Surgery: A time of inner healing.

Swamp: Caution.

Sweater: A false sense of comfort.

Swimsuit: The Lord sending out and commissioning. A time of rest.

Sword: The word of God. Prophecy. Declaration.

Syringe: Fear. Anxiety. Healing.

T

Table: Community. Connection in relationships.

Tag: Important information. The Lord bringing understanding of identity.

Tail: Complacency. Settling for less (Deuteronomy 28:13).

Tape: Unity. Partnership. Looking for a quick fix.

Tarp: The Lord's protection. Spiritual accountability.

Tattoo: Being marked by the Lord.

Unlocking the Language of Dreams

Taxi: A ministry or person an individual may be partnered with for a season.

Tea: Healing. A time of cleansing.

Tear: Inner healing. The Lord exposing wounds of the heart.

Teeth: Knowledge. Understanding. Wisdom.

Television: Increase of influence. Unhealthy dependency. Escapism.

Temple: The physical body. Holiness. A call to be set apart.

Tent: A wilderness season. Adventure.

Thermos: The Lord preserving something for a later time.

Throat: An individual's level of feeling as though they have a voice or a say in their life.

Throne: God's glory. God's authority over the nations.

Thunder: God's word. God's declaration.

Tiara: A revelation of daughtership from the Father. Revelation of royal identity in Christ.

Tie: Promotion. A spirit of excellence.

Tightrope: A call to take risk. Living too close to the edge. Caution. Compromise.

Dream Interpretation Dictionary

Tire: Holy Spirit. The things that carry an individual's ministry.

Toilet: The Lord bringing cleansing.

Tomb: Something coming to an end. Leaving a past season behind.

Tombstone: Something coming to an end. Leaving a past season behind.

Tongue: Speaking the word of the Lord. The prophetic ministry. Gossip. Lies.

Tool: A spiritual gift (1 Corinthians 12), anointing, skill or ability.

Tooth: Knowledge. Understanding. Wisdom.

Tooth (Wisdom): Wisdom.

Toothbrush: The Lord refining knowledge, understanding or wisdom.

Tornado: Transition. Realignment. Winds of change. Someone the Lord is using to bring change. The call of a forerunner. Reformation. Chaos. Warning. Caution. Plans of the enemy.

Toupee: A false perception of identity.

Tower: A specific ministry. Demonic stronghold. Bondage.

Toy: Symbol of childhood. Innocence. Childlikeness.

Unlocking the Language of Dreams

Trail - Symbol of an individual's life. A specific season.

Treasure: A gift from the Lord. Provision from the Lord.

Tree: Specific leaders. Principalities.

Trigger: A pivotal decision.

Truck: Business anointing. The realm of finances. Wealth.

Trunk: Extra baggage. Bondage.

Trumpet: God's prophetic word.

Turtle: Humility. Wisdom. Protection. A time of hiddenness. A seasoned leader. A father or mother of the faith.

Tuxedo: A monumental season of life. A milestone in life.

U

Umbrella: The Lord's protection. Spiritual accountability.

Underpants: Shame. The sense of feeling embarrassed or exposed.

Dream Interpretation Dictionary

Universe: The mysteries of God.

Uphill: A test from the Lord. A specific circumstance.

Urinal: A time of cleansing.

V

Vaccine: Caution. Fear. Anxiety.

Vacuum: A time to focus on cleaning up a mess, whether that is in a ministry, business, circumstances, relationships, etc.

Vault: Keeping something hidden for a season. Protecting the things of the Lord.

Valley: A season of training. Preparation for promise. A time of God healing the soul.

Vehicle: Ministry.

Veil: Something that the Lord of preserving for a later time. Something hindering connection with the heart of God. Hidden sin.

Vein: The blood of Jesus. Different streams of society (government, business, the arts and entertainment, media, the church, the education system or family.)

Vest: Anointing. Mantle. Calling.

Violin: Musical anointing. Creativity. Worship. A time of self-expression.

Volcano: The power of God. A move of the Spirit of God. A heart wound manifesting.

Vulture: Something about to come to an end. The enemy trying to thwart God's plans.

W

Wagon: Support for what the Lord has called someone to build.

Wall: The Lord's protection. Something hindering connection with the heart of God.

Wallet: The realm of finances. Wealth. Identity.

Wand: Witchcraft. Manipulation. Control. Spirit of Jezebel.

Wardrobe: A storehouse of different giftings, anointings, callings, mantles, skills and abilities.

Warrior: Spiritual warfare. A call to stand amidst opposition.

Warship: Spiritual warfare.

Washer: A time of cleansing.

Washroom: A time of cleansing.

Waste: Something that God wants to get rid of in an individual's life.

Water: Holy Spirit. The anointing over an individual's life.

Water (Rushing): Season of acceleration. Anointing flowing.

Water (Still): Peace. Intimacy. An anointing that has gone stagnant and unused.

Weakness: Lack of spiritual food. Lack of confidence. Lack of rest.

Weapon: Weapon of warfare. Gifts, anointings, skills or abilities.

Weariness: Lack of rest. Fatigue.

Weasel: Manipulation. Lies.

Weather Forecasting: God calling an individual to discern their season. A season shift.

Web: Lies. A trap from the enemy.

Weeds: Hindrances to prevent ministry from flourishing. Unhealthy relationships. Trials that the Lord permits to bring maturity.

Whale: Humility. Meekness.

Unlocking the Language of Dreams

Wheel: Holy Spirit. The things that carry an individual's ministry.

Wheelbarrow: Support for what the Lord has called someone to build.

Wheelchair: An area in life where someone does not feel capable.

Whispering: The voice of the Lord. Gossip. Lies.

White (Positive side): God. Purity. Clarity. Goodness. Faithfulness.

White (Negative side): Religious spirit.

White Hair: Wisdom.

Wife: The Bride of Christ. Literal wife.

Wig: A false perception of identity.

Wind: Change. Moving from one place to another. Holy Spirit.

Wine: Anointing. Miracles. Signs and wonders (John 2).

Wineskin (Old): An old system or way of hosting the things of God.

Wineskin (New): A new system or way of hosting the things of God.

Window: Revelation. A foot-in for the enemy.

Wings: Angels. The Lord's protection. (Psalm 91:4). The ability to rise above circumstances.

Winter: Purity. Holiness. A wilderness season. A time where God is growing character.

Wisdom Tooth: Wisdom.

Wolf: Prayer. Intercession. A wolf in sheep's clothing. Warning.

World: God's global plan. A worldly way of thinking.

Wound: Wound of the heart. Caution. Warning. Fear. Anxiety. Insecurity.

Wrinkles: Wisdom.

X

X-ray: God revealing what is occurring in someone's heart.

Y

Yawning: Lack of rest. Fatigue. Complacency.

Yard: Symbol of an individual's life. Symbol of an

individual's childhood.

Yeast: Something that is harmful that God wants removed (Matthew 16:6). Religious spirit.

Yellow (Positive side): Childlikeness. Faith. Courage. Bravery. Hope. Knowledge. The ministry of teaching.

Yellow (Negative side): Cowardice. Doubt. Passivity.

Yoke (That is Light): A burden from the Lord.

Yoke (That is Heavy): A burden not from the Lord. A significant or weighty calling.

Z

Zeal: Passion for God.

Zombie: The enemy trying to resurrect what God has already taught someone to overcome.

Zoo: Different giftings and anointings working together. Different aspects of an individual's identity or calling where they do not feel freedom.

Made in the USA
Lexington, KY
26 May 2019